P9-AOT-757

STUDIES IN HISTORY, ECONOMICS AND PUBLIC LAW

Edited by the
FACULTY OF POLITICAL SCIENCE
OF COLUMBIA UNIVERSITY

NUMBER 450

INTERDEPARTMENTAL COMMITTEES IN THE NATIONAL ADMINISTRATION

BY

MARY TRACKETT REYNOLDS

INTERDEPARTMENTAL COMMITTEES
IN THE
NATIONAL ADMINISTRATION

BY

MARY TRACKETT REYNOLDS

AMS PRESS
NEW YORK

COLUMBIA UNIVERSITY
STUDIES IN THE
SOCIAL SCIENCES

450

The Series was formerly known as *Studies in History, Economics and Public Law.*

Reprinted with the permission of Columbia University Press
From the edition of 1939, New York
First AMS EDITION published 1968
Manufactured in the United States of America

Library of Congress Catalogue Card Number: 68-58618

AMS PRESS, INC.
New York, N.Y. 10003

To

MOTHER

WITH LOVE

PREFACE

THE period on which this study is focussed primarily involves the years 1933 to 1937, or, roughly, the first administration of Franklin D. Roosevelt. Many of the committees which were appointed between 1933 and 1937 have now completed their tasks and have disbanded. Others are still functioning. Moreover, a number of interdepartmental committees now in active operation were appointed before Franklin Roosevelt took office, some of them as long as 15 or 20 years before. Still other committees, some of them of considerable importance, have been appointed since 1937. In a word, we are dealing here with an extremely fluent aspect of administration. Any period selected for study would necessarily be somewhat arbitrary. This book will deal only with those interdepartmental committees which functioned actively between 1933 and 1937, regardless of when they were appointed or whether they have now been abolished.

The reader's indulgence must be asked with regard to the many passages in the study which show the awkwardness of trying to pin down situations essentially dynamic. The description of a committee's activity at any given time is subject to change along lines which cannot always be accurately forecast. Even more confusing to the reader, perhaps, are my efforts to bring my material up to date in the face of the administrative reorganizations continually taking place in the national government. The personnel of interdepartmental committees changes continually, and the agencies represented on particular committees may overnight be reorganized, absorbed into other agencies, or even abolished. This sort of change is bound to take place in precisely those areas of administration in which coordination is needed. The use of integrating machinery, such as the interdepartmental committee, itself implies a need for readjustment of administrative relationships.

I am under obligation to Columbia University and the faculty of Political Science, for the grant of a University Fellowship in Public Law during 1936-37; also to the faculty of Barnard College, and the Women's Organization for National Prohibition Reform, for the grant of a Public Service Fellowship in 1937-38.

To Thomas H. Eliot, to Professor Alvin Hansen, and to Professor Fritz Morstein Marx, my thanks are due for invaluable assistance with portions of the study. I am greatly indebted to Professor Schuyler C. Wallace, who first suggested the study, and to Professor Lindsay Rogers, for their patience in reading and criticizing the entire manuscript. It is a pleasure to express my gratitude to Professor Arthur W. Macmahon, under whose immediate direction the study was prepared, for continual guidance and encouragement.

MARY T. REYNOLDS

CAMBRIDGE, MASSACHUSETTS,
NOVEMBER 20, 1938.

TABLE OF CONTENTS

CHAPTER I

THE SOURCES OF INTERDEPARTMENTAL RELATIONSHIPS

THE administrative operations of the federal government are parcelled out among a multitude of bureaus, commissions, authorities and similar agencies, most of which are placed in departments roughly organized by major objectives. With the increasing volume and extent of governmental operations, a perfectly functional arrangement becomes impossible. Thus, for example, we have a Public Health Service in one department and a Biological Survey unit in another. Suppose the former emphasizes the need for controlling mosquitoes by draining swamp lands; the latter may prefer to preserve marsh areas as wild life habitations. Again, in the development of almost any river basin, a variety of alternatives arise to confuse governmental policy. One bureau may view the river as a source of potable drinking water, another as a means of sewage disposal, while still a third may be interested in its potentialities for recreational development. One bureau may wish to use the river for power, another for navigation. Thus one problem may touch the work of administrative units in several departments.

But if governmental action is to be effective, some degree of consistency, some compromise among conflicting preferences, must be achieved. The government must take all possible alternatives into consideration in shaping its policies. Its decisions cannot be made in isolation, nor in the abstract. As a practical matter of reconciling conflicts, consultation among the officials in different administrative units is essential. Inevitably, then, numerous specialized contacts cut horizontally across the lines of command at those points where several departments are concerned in a particular problem.

Moreover, the growing preoccupation of government with economic problems increases the long-range implications of every administrative act, with the benefits of coordination resulting at many points. The AAA tried to improve agricultural conditions by raising the prices of farm products. The government was then faced with the effects of this policy on the industrial worker who had to purchase farm products. Nor are the effects of a policy always so obvious. Government act A concerning agriculture, and government act B relating to business, both set in motion in the community a complicated chain of events in which it soon becomes difficult to trace the effects of specific decisions. The policies operate in almost subterranean fashion, submerged beneath routine economic activity, until finally the two policies may cross each other and serious conflict may occur.

It is part of the task of government to foresee these long-range effects so far as possible, and to relate immediate decision to long-run thinking. Planning and research are thus an essential part of administration. Government needs to devise machinery which will organize intelligence and bring it to bear on problems of economic and social policy. Staff work should be done by agencies able to take an over-all viewpoint, to see the administration as a whole. Consultative relationships should be established between departments, to apply the comprehensive design to specific operations.

Further, even should departments succeed fully in the scheme of coordination through hierarchy, the need for interdepartmental relationships would remain. Even supposing that bureaus might be grouped on a perfectly functional basis, still there are certain interdepartmental contacts inherent in the nature of unified administrative organization. Such interdepartmental relationships may perhaps best be exemplified by alluding to the functions of the head of an administrative department.

In the formulation and execution of policy, the head of a department in the national government has a multiple responsibility. He is, of course, answerable for the major decisions on which his agency's operations rest. In addition, however, the department head has certain external responsibilities.

First, the department head will naturally observe the effects of action elsewhere in the government upon the performance of tasks particularly assigned to his department. If his department deals specifically with certain well-defined occupational groups, the department head is expected to take what steps he can to see that the interests of such groups are not damaged by the actions of other governmental agencies. For example, when the NRA set out to raise price levels in industry, in 1933, the Secretary of Labor immediately expressed concern that wage levels should rise proportionately. Likewise, the Secretary of Agriculture became the focus of anxiety lest the prices of finished products be advanced unduly. In the sessions of an interdepartmental Cabinet Committee on Prices, the Secretary of Agriculture urged that National Recovery Administration code provisions fixing regular hours should not apply to the perishable food industry.

In those departments which are not directly concerned with occupational elements, the department head still has the obligation to see that the activities of his department are not hindered or nullified by action elsewhere in the government. The activities of the War and Navy departments in planning for national defense might be seriously affected by the activities of the Commerce Department in establishing commercial airports and the Treasury Department in designating certain commercial airports as points of entry into the United States.

Nor is the department head's responsibility to observe the impinging effects of other departmental policies always the negative sort of watchfulness that merely prevents obstruction or duplication. For example, the State Department's action in establishing international trans-oceanic air routes would be of interest to the Post Office Department as a means of improving airmail services.

Second, the department head has an individual consultative relationship to the committees of Congress, and to the administration as a whole. Department heads have at least a tacit obligation to furnish information to the committees of Congress, to the President, and to their fellow administrators. In order to furnish such information, the department head has two alternatives. Either he must be familiar with the details of the operations of the bureaus within his department, or he must delegate to a subordinate the responsibility of furnishing the information. The department head has the choice of obtaining information through memoranda or permitting the official engaged in the activity to supply the data in direct consultation with the agency seeking information. Interdepartmental relationships often arise from such situations. When the Public Works Administration began to operate, Secretary Ickes asked the Secretary of Labor to appoint a labor advisory board, to advise the Public Works Administrator on general matters of labor policy in his organization.[1]

Third, the heads of the ten executive departments are members of the President's Cabinet, and in this capacity it is desirable that each shall have points of view on the general problems and general policies of the administration as a whole. In a sense, the President's Cabinet may be considered the original interdepartmental committee. Thus the Cabinet might discuss a federal housing policy, not in the narrow terms of each department's participation, but with reference to the Administration's general objectives. The discussion might contrast the prospects

1 The obligation of administrative departments to furnish information to committees of Congress may also result in interdepartmental relationships. When the congressional committees on military and naval affairs are preparing legislation for national defense, they will inevitably call upon the Departments of War and Navy to describe the country's condition and requirements. It is the duty of administrators in these departments to respond with full and accurate information. But this does not mean that the Secretary of War and Secretary of the Navy personally present this data. In almost all cases, the officers in charge of army and navy planning bureaus appear in person before Congress to furnish the data required. (Occasionally there are exceptions, as when Secretary of War Elihu Root personally supported the bill creating the General Staff, in 1903.) Although each of the defense departments has its own committee in both House and Senate, the army and navy are sufficiently aware of the need for a unified plan of national defense to make a practice of working together on joint planning committees.

offered by a policy of granting subsidies to private concerns with the implications of a policy of actual public construction of low-cost housing.

A further type of interdepartmental activity arises out of the need for coordination created by central management of personnel, procurement, statistics, and similar institutional or housekeeping functions.[2] In the interests of unified administrative action, the housekeeping phases of administration are better handled by central management than by the departments independently. Central management, however, necessitates interdepartmental contacts. The personnel director must be aware on the one hand of the activities of personnel officers in other departments, and on the other hand of the work of the Civil Service Commission. Conversely, if the Civil Service Commission is to be a genuine organ of central personnel administration, it will have to maintain constant contact with the departmental personnel officers.[3]

Three sources of interdepartmental relationships have now been distinguished. First, interdepartmental contacts arise through the imperfections of the functional type of organization and the consequent necessity for consultation on problems which are not wholly within the scope of any single department. Second, interdepartmental contacts are often a necessary phase of administrative planning, for they offer a means of anticipating possible conflicts arising from the long-range effects of governmental activity in economic matters. Third, certain types of interdepartmental relationships are inherent in the nature of unified administrative action. The conclusion seems inescapable that interdepartmental contacts will always

2 *Cf.* W. F. Willoughby, *Principles of Public Administration* (Brookings Institution, Washington, D. C., 1927), pp. 45-6.

3 See p. 92 below. See also President's Committee on Administrative Management, *Report and Special Studies* (Washington, D. C., 1937), p. 63, for an account of the Council of Personnel Administration. On the interdepartmental structure for federal procurement activities, see Charles A. Beard, *American Leviathan*, pp. 370-375.

be indispensable. Interdepartmental relationships are a necessary, proper, and permanent feature of administration in the national government.

Clearly, then, the intelligent and systematic conduct of interdepartmental relationships is one of the major problems of administration. Many of these relationships are best handled informally.[4] When important problems or policies are reached, however, a telephone call may not be sufficient to bring about agreement among the departments involved. Among the techniques which have been found useful for the conduct of interdepartmental negotiations is the interdepartmental committee.[5] A study of the interdepartmental committee in the national government of the United States should be illuminating in a dual sense. First, it should furnish specific factual information regarding methods of coordination in the federal government. Second, it should sharpen the accuracy of our ideas regarding the nature of the consultative process in public administration.

As part of the coordinating machinery of the national government, the interdepartmental committee has one general objective: the cooperative framing of the bases for administrative action. There is one general criterion by which its success may be estimated: the degree to which the committee's decisions, whether positive or negative, are adopted as the basis for action in the participating departments. These broad statements cover the whole contribution of the interdepartmental committee to administrative coordination. In order to study this contribution, however, it is necessary to be more specific. We must consider particular committees in the light of the problems they have faced. We must also consider the level of administrative

4 See W. Ivor Jennings, *Cabinet Government* (Macmillan Co., New York City, 1936), p. 104.

5 Of course the interdepartmental committee is not the only device used for coordination. See L. Gulick, "Notes on the Theory of Organization," in *Papers on the Science of Administration* (Institute of Public Administration, New York City, 1937), pp. 6 *et seq.*

policy with which they have dealt. Consequently, it will be profitable to examine the interdepartmental committee under three headings.[6]

In a first category, interdepartmental committees have actually taken part in the formulation of the Administration's economic and social objectives. For purposes of this study we may call these committees exploratory. Perhaps the committee has investigated proposals for new legislation, and drafted a tentative bill. Such was the task of the Committee on Economic Security.[7] Again, the committee's work may have been exploratory in a broader sense, not directly related to legislative proposals. The National Resources Committee is one example, and the National Advisory Committee on Aeronautics another.[8] The success or failure of such groups cannot be judged solely on the basis of whether the policy which they recommend is adopted. Even when a committee's recommendations are given effect, the element of time must be considered. Where plans are long-run in character, it may take a generation or so to afford a satisfactory basis for appraisal. Subsidiary criteria must therefore be set up to estimate the quality of the committee's work. Has the committee unearthed all the significant facts? Has it grasped all the implications? Do its conclusions reflect a spirit of departmentalism or are they truly an over-all policy based on the viewpoints of several departments? Has the group revealed creative intelligence in attacking the problem?

In a second category, other committees are set up to construct procedures through which an announced policy can be

6 For convenience in analyzing interdepartmental committees some sort of grouping is necessary. The categories set up are merely tentative; no rigid classification is intended or implied.

7 See p. 28 below.

8 For a description of the work of these two committees, see the various reports and other publications issued by the National Resources Committee, and the *Annual Report* issued by the National Advisory Committee on Aeronautics.

given practical effect. The broad outlines of such a policy may be revealed in legislative enactment or administrative order, which may both state the government's major objectives and also indicate in a general way the methods by which they are to be attained. There will still remain, however, the task of framing the working policy of the operating agencies. " Law . . . at best is a coarse network, whose interstices must be filled by administrative action of one kind or another—an order in council . . . a rule, an order of individual application, an administrative decision." [9] It is clearly advantageous to have such administrative rules framed by the agencies which are going to give effect to the policy.

In the chapters that follow we shall see how interdepartmental committees have been used at this second level of policy-formation. We may conveniently call them coordinating committees for the functional or service aspects of administrative policy. How can we judge the effectiveness of these groups? First of all, by the degree of genuine consultation that has been achieved. Has the policy really been evolved from an exchange of ideas, a blending of viewpoints? If the committee's recommendations, whether negative or positive, are not given effect by the participating departments, there is a strong presumption that the committee has not been successful.

However, committees of this second type represent three slightly different sets of circumstances. First, responsibility for the activity in most cases will be lodged in a single department, and other agencies whose work impinges on the particular problem will be invited to express their viewpoints in an advisory capacity. In such instances it is difficult to set up an objective criterion for judging whether the committee has really been an effective coordinating device. The success of the program does not depend entirely upon the committee. The decisive ele-

9 Leonard D. White, " The Meaning of Principles in Public Administration," *Frontiers of Public Administration* (University of Chicago Press, 1936), p. 14.

ment may have been the work of the department responsible for the program. Have the interests represented on the committee been given a substantial hearing? This is the main point to consider in examining interdepartmental groups in which one department is responsible for the program. The Executive Committee on Commercial Policy and the Trade Agreements committees are typical examples.[10]

A second, and somewhat different sort of functional coordination is found where several departments are individually responsible for separate parts of a program. Their policies must be integrated or there will be no concerted action. Consequently each will be represented on an interdepartmental committee which will in effect direct the program. We may roughly describe the interdepartmental committees conforming to the first pattern as federal in character, while those which follow the second pattern may be said to be essentially confederate in their nature. The effectiveness of these latter committees is clearly revealed in the development of the program under their control. Has the committee been able to come to agreement? Have the departments consistently accepted and followed the committee's decisions? The method used in designating certain cities as airports of entry into the United States is typical of this kind of coordination. Three agencies have been made responsible by statute for the activity: the Customs Bureau of the Treasury Department, the Immigration Service of the Labor Department, and the Bureau of Air Commerce of the Commerce Department (now merged in the Civil Aeronautics Authority). A fourth, the Department of Agriculture, though not mentioned in the law, is vitally interested from the standpoint of plant and animal quarantine inspections. The U. S. Public Health Service, of the Treasury Department, also participates in an informal way. The five agencies operate together through the Interdepartmental Committee for Designation of Airports of Entry. Similarly, the health and welfare activities

10 See p. 47 below.

of the government have been integrated to a considerable extent by the Interdepartmental Committee on Health and Welfare.[11]

In a third set of situations, several departments will be engaged in activities that are similar or related. Though hardly part of an articulated program, they find it desirable, simply as members of the same administrative family, to keep informed about each others' work. Otherwise their activities may overlap and they may duplicate each other. Or one agency may take action which conflicts with the policies of the others or with the general objectives of the Administration. An interdepartmental committee may be used in such instances simply as a convenient method of exchanging information and ideas. Committees which are mainly discussion groups are difficult to evaluate. One should not overlook the educational value of the systematic association of administrators from various agencies. It broadens the individual's outlook; it should lessen the spirit of departmentalism. Nevertheless, one should not overestimate the value of contacts of this sort. Those administrators who show a spirit of cooperation in interdepartmental discussion groups probably show that quality in all their activities. It is doubtful whether membership on this type of committee has ever changed the viewpoints of a convinced departmental isolationist. Moreover, interdepartmental meetings with only a nebulous assignment can be first-class time-wasters. "It is sometimes forgotten that the cost of any committee is the combined salaries of its members for the time spent at the committee or preparing for it." [12] The key question is, therefore, how far the committee has been able to center the discussion upon the vital aspects of the problem, to minimize duplication of activity, and to adopt a formula which will be accepted by all the agencies involved. The problems typically encountered by interdepartmental discussion groups may per-

11 See p. 70 below.

12 L. Urwick, "Organization as a Technical Problem", in *Papers on the Science of Administration* (Institute of Public Administration, New York City, 1937), p. 83.

haps be illustrated by reference to the experience of the Central Housing Committee.[13]

In addition to the exploration of new policies and the integration of functional activity, coordination is necessary in a third stage in the development of the administrative processes of government. The procedures used in connection with personnel management or purchasing are typical of those auxiliary technical operations which are generally called institutional or housekeeping activities. The criteria set up to evaluate the functional coordinating committees may also be applied to the committees which coordinate the housekeeping aspects of administration. Has the committee dealt with the vital points at issue between departments? Has it been able to agree on joint action at the disputed points? Has its action been given effect in subsequent operations? Some of these committees are borderline cases in which the activity is primarily one which facilitates administrative operations, yet one in which a certain amount of policy-making is involved. The allocation of radio wavelengths to departmental broadcasting stations is one example.[14] Coordination of statistical services is another.[15]

The student of public administration is first of all interested in knowing what kinds of administrative endeavor are properly the concern of an interdepartmental committee. The chapters in Part I will thus be concerned with the interdepartmental committee from the viewpoint of its objectives. We can best estimate the usefulness of committees for certain types of tasks if we examine some of the uses to which committees have typically been put. Each of the three major categories which have just been described will in turn be illustrated with brief case studies of typical committees. In the second place, certain problems are common to all interdepartmental committees, regardless of their specific objectives. A discussion of

13 See p. 78 below.

14 See p. 117 below.

15 See p. 94 below.

these common problems must be based on a cross-sectional view of a number of interdepartmental committees. Part II of the study, therefore, will treat the interdepartmental committee from the standpoint of methods employed in its establishment and subsequent operations.

Before turning to an intensive examination of the interdepartmental committee, the scope of the interdepartmental problem may be briefly summarized. The study of public administration is a study of human relationships. Although the hierarchical form of organization and the meeting of minds in consultation are sometimes thought to be contrasting principles, in reality they are complementary techniques of administration. Effective management requires a wide use of consultative procedures to instill a sense of purpose throughout the administrative hierarchy. This process, which is called coordination, is accomplished primarily through staff agencies and conference mechanisms. The former imply the furnishing of information and advice to the chief administrator; the latter imply a cooperative framing of working policies. In the national government, interdepartmental relationships are a necessary, proper and permanent feature of administration. Most of these relationships are informal. When important problems are confronted, however, interdepartmental contacts are often formalized in a committee. Interdepartmental committees may be grouped under three major headings. The first is the exploratory or research committee, the second the functional coordinating committee, and the third the institutional coordinating committee.

PART I

OBJECTIVES

CHAPTER II

EXPLORATORY COMMITTEES

The exploratory committee is one phase of the attempt to organize intelligence and bring it to bear on the framing of governmental policy. Exploratory committees are one type of machinery for thinking. The distinguishing characteristic of the exploratory committee is that it draws together administrative officials from two or more departments or independent agencies for the purpose of research. Sometimes the committee will concern itself directly with the framing of legislative proposals. In other instances it will investigate matters which may possibly become the subject of legislation but on which legislative action is not immediately contemplated. It is the task of this chapter to describe a committee which has formulated legislative requests. First, however, it will be profitable to enumerate briefly the considerations which lead to administrative participation in the legislative process, and to set forth some of the reasons why several departments may be consulted in planning a legislative proposal.

Manifestly, administrative officials in modern governments cannot be excluded from the framing of policy, either in theory or in practice. First, it is clear that only those who have had actual administrative experience can judge whether legislative proposals are practicable and workable. Second, the subject-matter of legislation today is complicated and technical. A detailed expert inquiry is an essential prerequisite of most important legislative measures. Very frequently the specialized knowledge which is needed for a particular piece of legislation can be found within the administration. It may be that some governmental bureau has been engaged in research along just those lines on which information is needed. Moreover, it often happens that governmental officials, quite aside from their ordinary tasks, have expert knowledge of some phase of the activity under consideration.

Third, there is often a strong controversial element in modern legislation. It is often found desirable to supplement the work of administrators in exploring legislative proposals with opinions from advisory groups of scientists, scholars, business men and the like. Non-governmental advisers are useful in a dual capacity. Because they are detached from the regular departments of government, they secure a certain amount of objectivity in the consideration of the problem. At the same time, if properly chosen they secure the very opposite of detachment by presenting an opportunity to sound out the clashing participants. But there is no special virtue merely in the act of consulting outside opinion. Indeed, if the attempt is made to use a group of non-governmental individuals merely as a sounding board, to assure favorable publicity rather than to receive the considered opinions of the persons consulted, the effects may even be disastrous to the proposed legislation. The testimony of non-governmental advisers will be most fruitful when it has been intelligently assimilated with the research and advice furnished by administrators. Consequently, an administrative agency sometimes furnishes a convenient focus for the work of such advisory groups.

Whether administrative officials take the initiative in proposing legislation, or whether they are called upon to offer advice and criticism on bills initiated by congressional committees, in either case there is need for unifying the administration's legislative requests. In the formulation of an integrated program of legislative requests, interdepartmental consultation is often found desirable. First, it is highly advisable to reconcile the conflicting viewpoints of departments before the proposals are submitted to Congress. If the proposals of different agencies conflict with each other, they tend to confuse rather than enlighten the congressional mind. Bureau chiefs then appear before congressional committees in the role of rival lobbyists rather than impersonal advisers. "In a considerable number of cases the end result has been the defeat of legislation which probably would have passed had the different points of view of the interested administrative departments been adjusted in advance of the introduction of the proposal in Congress. . . . Though the ultimate decision in all such conflicts rests with Congress, its work is hindered by bickering and conflicts between departments." [1]

Second, the attempt to think through the policies represented in legislative proposals often requires consultation between two or more departments. "The financial, international and other effects and implications of all such proposals should be carefully examined, and before any attempt is made to interest the Congress in the enactment of these proposals into law all probable consequences should be weighed judiciously, to prevent creating more serious problems than the conditions which it is sought to remedy." [2]

Third, the search for facts in preliminary research often leads to consultation of fact-finding agencies or specialists in several departments. Both the Tariff Commission and the Department of Commerce are important sources of information on foreign trade. Statistics on housing are collected by more than 30 federal bureaus.[3] Examples could be multiplied indefinitely.

Perhaps the outstanding example of the present administration's efforts to plan legislative recommendations by means of an interdepartmental committee was the Committee on Economic Security. This committee was set up to deal with a specific problem and was disbanded upon completion of its task. By examining the origins, operations, and effectiveness of the Committee on Economic Security, we may draw from its experience some conclusions regarding the general usefulness of such a device for integrating legislative proposals.

1 Edwin E. Witte, "The Preparation of Proposed Legislative Measures by Administrative Departments," in *Report and Special Studies*, President's Committee on Administrative Management (Washington, D. C., 1937), pp. 362-369.

2 *Ibid.*, p. 362.

3 Central Housing Committee, *Activities and Organization of Federal Agencies Concerned with Housing* (Washington, D. C., 1936).

The Comittee on Economic Security[4]

In 1934, social security had begun to be recognized as a genuinely national problem. Its ramifications were not yet fully realized. Eighteen states had set up old-age pension systems. However, 25 states were without any such laws, and five had ineffective optional systems. Moreover, the financial burden of paying adequate benefits was becoming too great for many

4 The Committee on Economic Security was selected for detailed analysis on three grounds. First, it was concerned with an important piece of legislation. Second, its operations from the time it was organized to the time it disbanded are easily traceable. Third, in its objectives, structure, and the general outlines of its activity, this committee is typical of those interdepartmental groups which fall within the classification of exploratory committees.

Other exploratory committees, interdepartmental in composition, which were in operation between 1932 and 1936 are as follows:

Transportation Legislation Committee.
Shipping Policy Committee.
Interdepartmental Ocean-Mail Contract Committee.
Interdepartmental Committee on Stock Exchange Regulation.
Farm Tenancy Committee.
Cabinet Committee to Review the Nationality Laws.
Interdepartmental Committee on Copyright.
Cabinet Committee to Study Prices.
National Advisory Health Council.
National Advisory Committee for Aeronautics.
National Research Council.
Interdepartmental Committee on Prohibition Repeal.
Communications Coordinating Committee.
Committee to Consider Tonnage Tax.
Committee on Federal Incorporation.
Commerce Research Committee of the Executive Board of NRA.
Occupational Research Studies Committee.
Committee on Increase in Production and Employment.
Textile Foundation Inc.
Committee to Cooperate with the Upper Monongahela Valley Planning Council.
National Forest Reservation Committee.
Mississippi River Commission.
Interdepartmental Board on Great Lakes and St. Lawrence River Project.
National Power Policy Committee.
National Resources Committee.

of the states.[5] A movement arose for federal grants-in-aid to encourage state old-age pension systems, and the Dill-Connery bill was introduced in 1933-34 as a first step in this direction. However, President Roosevelt wished to combine old-age pensions with a general unified program for federal social security. Unemployment insurance was to be included in the program. Unemployment insurance schemes had been enacted in Wisconsin and had been introduced in the legislatures of at least twenty states. The Wagner-Lewis bill, introduced in the national Congress in 1934, was designed to encourage states to enact unemployment insurance laws. This bill had been drafted in the Department of Labor. It did not receive strong Presidential support in Congress, however, for the reason again that a unified federal program was anticipated. Many elements and agencies were involved, and until these had been unified the President would not give strong support to any measure.

To be genuinely comprehensive, a program of social security would necessarily include elements other than unemployment insurance and old-age pensions. Provisions for child welfare, and maternal and child health services might be essential. Security for the blind claimed consideration. All these problems had been approached by state governments and local communities, with varying degrees of success. After 1930, financial disintegration of state and local governments had brought a gradual decline or even abandonment of such programs. It was time for the federal government to step in, if the people's health and security were to be maintained.[6]

In a special message to Congress on June 8, 1934, President Roosevelt expressed his intention to recommend to the next session of Congress, "Additional measures of protection

5 For fuller discussion of the social security movement in the United States, see Paul H. Douglas, *Social Security in the United States* (McGraw-Hill, New York City, 1936).

6 For a more detailed account of the events leading up to the appointment of the Committee on Economic Security, see Paul H. Douglas, *Social Security in the United States.*

against the major vicissitudes of life which result in destitution and dependency for many individuals." As a first step toward this end, the President created the Committee on Economic Security by executive order on June 29, 1934.[7] As members of the Committee he appointed the Secretary of Labor (chairman), the Secretary of the Treasury, the Attorney-General, the Secretary of Agriculture, and the Federal Emergency Relief Administrator. The Committee was given a broad mandate to study problems relating to the economic security of individuals. It was ordered to report its recommendations to the President not later than December 1, 1934.

The executive order which created the Committee on Economic Security also provided for the appointment of an Advisory Council, a Technical Board, and an Executive Director. The Advisory Council was to be composed of citizens not connected with the federal government, and was expected to advise the cabinet committee on problems of general policy. Appointments to the Council were made by the President. The membership finally included 23 business men, labor leaders, social workers, educators, editors, and other individuals.[8] The cabinet

7 Executive Order No. 6757, June 29, 1934.

8 The membership of the Advisory Council was as follows:
Frank P. Graham, president University of North Carolina (chairman).
Paul Kellogg, editor *The Survey* (vice chairman).
Gerard Swope, president General Electric Company.
Morris E. Leeds, president Leeds and Northrup.
Sam Lewisohn, vice president Miami Copper Company.
Walter C. Teagle, president Standard Oil Company of New Jersey.
Marion B. Folsom, assistant treasurer Eastman Kodak Co.
William Green, president American Federation of Labor.
George M. Harrison, president Brotherhood of Railway and Steamship Clerks.
Henry Ohl, Jr., president Wisconsin State Federation of Labor.
Paul Scharrenberg, secretary California State Federation of Labor.
Belle Sherwin, former president National League of Women Voters.
Grace Abbott, University of Chicago, former chief U. S. Children's Bureau.
Raymond Moley, editor *Today*.
George H. Nordlin, chairman grand trustees Fraternal Order of Eagles.

committee also set up seven advisory committees on special aspects of social security, composed of citizens who were specialists in public health and welfare work.[9]

The Technical Board was organized to bring into the machinery certain officials in various administrative departments who had shown some degree of interest in or special knowledge of social security problems. The executive order specified that the Board should consist of "qualified representatives selected from various departments and agencies of the Federal government." Appointments to the Technical Board were made by the cabinet committee.[10] Although the Technical

George Berry, president International Printing Pressmen and Assistants' Union.

John G. Winant, Governor of New Hampshire.

Mary Dewson, National Consumers League.

Louis J. Taber, master National Grange.

Father John A. Ryan, director Department of Social Action, National Catholic Welfare Conference.

Helen Hall, president National Federation of Settlements.

Joel D. Hunter, general superintendent United Charities of Chicago.

Elizabeth Morrissey, Notre Dame College, Baltimore, Md.

9 The Medical Advisory Committee, the Public Health Advisory Committee, the Hospital Advisory Board, the Dental Advisory Committee, the Advisory Committee on Public Employment and Public Assistance, and the Committee on Child Welfare. There was also a committee of actuarial consultants. For the list of members of these advisory committees, see Committee on Economic Security, *Report* (U. S. Government Printing Office, Washington, D. C., 1935), pp. 52-53.

10 The membership of the Technical Board was as follows:

Arthur J. Altmeyer, Second Assistant Secretary of Labor, chairman.

Thomas H. Eliot, Assistant Solicitor, Department of Labor.

Isador Lubin, Commissioner of Labor Statistics, Department of Labor.

Josephine Roche, Assistant Secretary of the Treasury.

Jacob Viner, Assistant to the Secretary of the Treasury.

Herman Oliphant, General Counsel, Treasury Department.

Aubrey Williams, Assistant Administrator, Federal Emergency Relief Administration.

Corrington Gill, Assistant Administrator, FERA.

H. B. Myers, Assistant Director of Research and Statistics, FERA.

Alexander Holtzoff, Assistant to the Attorney-General.

Board was designed as an instrument for drawing upon the information and experience of those federal agencies which had long been concerned with welfare problems, members of the Board were chosen for their usefulness as individuals rather than as a means of assuring representation of departmental points of view. In some cases the individual's usefulness arose partly from his position in an important fact-gathering agency and partly from his previous experience on coordinating committees; for example, Stuart Rice and Winfield Riefler had both been very active in the Central Statistical Board. In other instances the official had shown special interest in some aspect of social security; for example, Alvin Hansen, then chief economic analyst in the State Department, was the author of two studies of unemployment insurance problems.

Only three meetings of the full Technical Board were held, all during the first few weeks of its existence. Thereafter the Board functioned through an executive committee and five subcommittees. Winfield Riefler was made chairman of the executive committee, Walton Hamilton chairman of a subcommittee on medical problems, Alvin Hansen chairman of an unemployment insurance subcommittee, Winfield Riefler chairman of a subcommittee on unemployment insurance reserve funds, Murray Latimer chairman of an old-age security subcommittee, and Aubrey Williams chairman of a public employment and public assistance subcommittee. All recommendations formally made by the Executive Director were first presented by him to the executive committee and the appropriate sub-

Victor N. Valgren, Senior Agricultural Economist, Department of Agriculture.
Alvin H. Hansen, Chief Economic Analyst, State Department.
E. Willard Jensen, Executive Secretary, Business Advisory Council.
Winfield Riefler, Executive Director, Central Statistical Board.
Walton H. Hamilton, Chairman of Advisory Council, NRA.
H. A. Millis, Board Member, National Labor Relations.
William M. Leiserson, Chairman, National Mediation Board.
Murray W. Latimer, Board Member, National Mediation Board.
Otto Beyer, Labor Relations Director, Office of Federal Coordinator of Transportation.

committee of the Technical Board, where the recommendations were discussed and voted upon. After revision and approval by the Technical Board, the recommendations were submitted to the Committee on Economic Security. In addition to the approval of specific recommendations, the Technical Board submitted two comprehensive reports to the Committee on Economic Security, in October and November, 1934. Meetings of the executive committee and subcommittees of the Technical Board were held as often as four or five times a week between September, 1934 and March, 1935. During this period, daily informal conferences were the rule.

As Executive Director, the cabinet committee chose Dr. Edwin E. Witte, Professor of Economics at the University of Wisconsin. Dr. Witte was well qualified for the post on the grounds of expert knowledge of social security problems. He had served for several years on the Wisconsin State Unemployment Compensation Commission, and had helped to administer the Wisconsin Unemployment insurance law, the first law of its kind in the United States. In addition, Dr. Witte's years of experience as head of the Wisconsin Legislative Reference Library gave him an intimate knowledge of the necessary steps to be taken in framing an adequate legislative program. Moreover, Dr. Witte's personality, temperament and successful experience as an administrator especially equipped him to direct the study of social security legislation. These considerations are mentioned at the outset because the position of Director was of major importance in the preparation of social security legislation. As executive secretary both of the cabinet committee and the Technical Board, the Director was the energizing center of the research structure. He was also the focus for contact between the administration and Congress when the social security bill was being considered by committees in the House and Senate.

The Executive Director set up a small staff to sift the research reports and perform other executive duties. He also organized his own technical staff, which included seven small groups of research workers. Finally, he arranged for the preparation of numerous special studies and memoranda by students of social security in various parts of the United States. The accompanying chart shows the complete research structure.

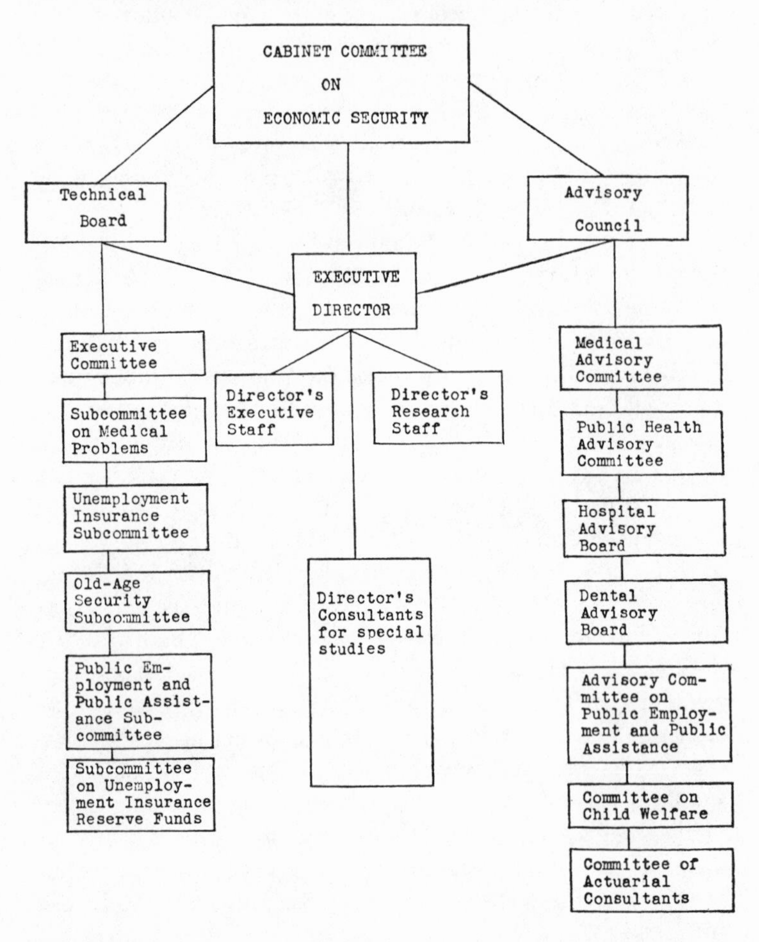

Although it is not possible to reconstruct the discussions of the Committee on Economic Security and its advisory groups, this can be approximated by examining certain problems upon which the discussions tended to concentrate. Basic cleavages of opinion can be distinguished. By following the divergent arguments through the masses of published material and unpublished manuscripts, the relative influence of various groups of opinion can be weighed. Similarly, it is possible also to evaluate the role played by the different kinds of levels of exploratory committees in the research structure.

Two major issues of policy confronted the committee.[11] First, what was to be the role of the national government? Should it work through the states, and if so how? Or should an outright national system of social security be established? Second, how costly a program should be adopted, and how should costs be distributed? Should a payroll tax or an income tax be used to raise funds? If a payroll tax were adopted, how should costs be distributed between workers and employers?

The most violent divergences of opinion occurred on the relative merits of a centralized national scheme of unemployment insurance versus a decentralized federal-state scheme.[12] Four lines of action were possible. An outright national plan might be adopted, disregarding state lines and providing direct federal benefits for unemployment insurance. Second, the scheme might be partially centralized, the federal government collecting the necessary taxes and furnishing the states 100% grants (i. e., block grants rather than matching subsidies or grants-in-aid) sufficient to cover the total amount of unemployment insurance benefits, while actual administration was conducted in the local units. Third, a still further step toward decentralization would make the states partially responsible for collection of funds by matching state appropriations with equal

11 Since the Cabinet Committee on Economic Security was the agency finally responsible for decisions, the words "committee" or "cabinet committee" will hereafter be used in connection with matters that are understood to be the concern of the research structure as a whole.

12 Since this is not a study of social security problems, no attempt will be made to discuss the relative merits of these proposals except as they entered into the discussions of the Committee on Economic Security. For a more detailed analysis of the various proposals, see Paul Douglas, *Social Security in the United States* (McGraw-Hill, New York City, 1936), pp. 28-68.

federal grants. Fourth, the tax offset system proposed in the Wagner-Lewis bill levied a 5% payroll tax on employers, providing that in states which passed a mandatory unemployment compensation law measuring up to certain minimum standards the contributions paid by employers to the state government would be credited as an offset against the federal tax.

A sharp controversy developed between proponents of the decentralized tax-offset plan and those favoring the scheme of centralized control through 100% block grants. The first group included the representatives of the Department of Labor, who had participated in the drafting of the original Wagner-Lewis bill, and also those members of the Technical Board and the Director's staff who favored the so-called Wisconsin plan of unemployment compensation. The principal dissenters were found on the Director's technical staff, but there was also a sharp division of opinion in the Technical Board and the Advisory Council. In the Technical Board, when the tax-offset plan was approved by the unemployment insurance subcommittee but rejected by the executive committee, a " Report on Major Alternative Plans " was prepared, which presented both sets of views for decision by the cabinet committee. The Advisory Council approved the block grants plan by a 9-7 vote (six members of the Council were absent, and one, Raymond Moley, did not vote) and several of its members publicly urged the adoption of the centralized scheme.[13] The Council's vote seems to have been influenced chiefly by Bryce Stewart, a member of the Director's staff.[14] However, officials on the Technical Board and the Executive Director convinced the cabinet committee of the soundness of the tax-offset plan, and the bill as finally submitted to Congress took this form.

13 The report of the Advisory Council is printed in *Hearings before the Committee on Ways and Means*, House of Representatives (74th Congress, 1st session, on HR 4120), pp. 882-896. See also the testimony of various members of the Council, in *Hearings before the Committee on Finance*, U. S. Senate (74th Congress, 1st session, on S. 1130).

14 See *New York Times*, October 14, 1934, pp. 22. Mr. Stewart is the head of Industrial Relations Counselors, Inc., of New York City.

A second major divergence of opinion appeared in connection with financial problems of the social security program. Disagreement arose in the Advisory Council over a 3% payroll tax which would limit unemployment compensation to 9 to 13 weeks of benefits after a three-week waiting period, versus a 5% tax which would furnish 30 weeks of benefits after a two-week waiting period. At least six members of the Council favored the 5% tax.[15] A minority of the Council also wished a federal tax on employees to help finance the program. This proposal was opposed by some officials in the Labor Department, and was dropped. The Advisory Council finally recommended the 3% tax, which was ultimately embodied in the bill recommended by the Committee on Economic Security.

The second financial issue concerned the old-age pension program. Two types of old-age assistance were included in the program. First, assistance was to be given to old people in need, benefits of this type to be paid from general tax sources. Second, a program of " insurance " was contemplated, in the form of retirement allowances payable as a matter of right to wage earners on retirement at a specified age, from funds to which they had contributed.[16] In connection with the second type of old-age assistance, it became clear that a maximum contribution equal to 10% of the worker's salary would be required to build up an adequate annuity. Controversy arose

15 The six members of the Advisory Council who favored this proposal were Paul Kellogg, William Green, Paul Scharrenberg, Henry Ohl, Jr., George M. Harrison, and Helen Hall—four labor leaders, an editor, and a social worker. The group who advocated the federal tax on employees was made up chiefly of the business men on the Council.

16 The original social security bill, as drafted by the Committee on Economic Security, embodied this idea. However, when the bill reached the House Ways and Means Committee, the provisions relating to old-age annuities were redrafted by Mr. Beaman, the House draftsman, in consultation with Thomas H. Eliot. Instead of the old age insurance fund, an old age reserve account was set up in the Treasury. The proceeds of the payroll tax were not allocated to the old age reserve account, nor to the payment of old age benefits; all provisions relating benefits to the payroll tax paid by employers and employees were eliminated, as well as all reference to contractual right to benefits.

almost immediately over alternative methods of raising the funds required to furnish adequate old-age annuities. In the first of the two major alternative plans, payroll taxes were to be collected in amounts sufficient to pay current benefits, the tax rates increasing slightly each year as the number of people receiving old age assistance increased. This "pay-as-you-go" plan would eventually run a deficit, as the number of pensioners increased beyond the practical limits of a payroll tax. The deficit might be met from general tax revenues or from the proceeds of some special tax; a tax on upper-bracket incomes was discussed but rejected. In the second major alternative plan, a payroll tax would be levied sufficient to pay current benefits and also, in the early years of the program, build up a surplus to be held in reserve. After a certain date, determined by the rate at which payroll contributions were adjusted to benefits, the annual interest on the reserve fund added to the amount received annually from the payroll tax would equal the amount of benefits to be paid out and the old-age assistance program would thus be made self-supporting.

For a time it seemed likely that the Treasury Department would file a minority report, disagreeing with the proposed financing of the old-age assistance program. The conservative element in the Treasury Department insisted that the payroll tax should be levied in such a way as not to alarm business and delay recovery. The conservative group opposed the tax on upper bracket incomes, and also opposed the creation of a large reserve fund on the grounds that it would encourage government spending. At the same time, the conservative group wished to have the plan made self-supporting rather than have a deficit created which would have to be met from general tax funds. Those who took the opposite view held that the payroll tax should be kept low in the interests of wage earners, the difference between contributions received and benefits paid out to be met by general taxation or by a special tax on upper-bracket incomes. The tax on upper-bracket incomes was dropped altogether and a compromise plan based primarily on the recommendations of the Director's staff was finally adopted and submitted to President Roosevelt by the Committee on Economic Security.

In the original recommendations of the Committee on Economic Security, provision was made for gradual application of the ultimate rates, beginning at one-half of one per cent on employees and the same on employers, for the five years 1937-1941 inclusive; an increase of one per cent was provided for the next five years, and a similar increase of one-half of one per cent every five years thereafter until a maximum of two and one-half per cent on employees and the same on employers would be reached in 1957 and continued thereafter. Under this plan a reserve of $14,000,000,000 would be created. After 1957 the difference between contributions and benefits would be covered by the interest on the reserve fund, but after 1965 a deficit would develop which would be met from general taxation. President Roosevelt, however, insisted that the rates of taxation and schedules of benefits be revised to make the plan entirely self-supporting. The Executive Director and the cabinet committee, guided by the Treasury Department, hastily revised their recommendations. The initial tax rate for the years 1937-1939 inclusive was raised to one per cent on employers and the same on employees; increases of one-half of one per cent were provided every three years until a maximum of three per cent on both employers and employees would be reached in 1949 and would continue thereafter. These new rates made the plan self-supporting at least until 1980; a reserve of $50,000,000,000 was contemplated, in contrast to the reserve of fourteen billion which would have been established by the original plan. When agreement had been reached and the President's approval secured, Secretary of the Treasury Morgenthau was selected to present the new tax and benefit rates to the House Ways and Means Committee on behalf of the entire Committee on Economic Security.

In general, disagreements were reconciled by open discussion. The cabinet committee met regularly, at weekly intervals, during the autumn and winter of 1934. The Executive Director supplied the cabinet committee with summaries of reports from his own technical staff, and also summarized for the committee the discussions of the Technical Board and the Advisory Council. Frequently the cabinet committee would request members of the advisory groups to appear at committee meetings for questioning. "The recommendations of the Committee," said its Director, "while based upon the preliminary proposals of the staff assigned to study the problem, evolved through an extended process of criticism and revision. Repeated conferences with the subcommittee on old-age security and with the executive committee of the Technical Board resulted in successive adjustments and amendments. The revised recommendations were presented to the Advisory Council and to experts outside the Committee's staff for criticism and suggestion. The conclusions . . . include, therefore, the contributions of many persons who with varied training and experience made a detailed analysis of the findings of the staff." [17] Disagreement was often bitter, and occasionally feeling ran so high that proponents of the centralized scheme denounced the advocates of the Wisconsin plan as biased, and some members of the two factions were scarcely on speaking terms.[18] The conflict is reflected in the hearings before the congressional committees.[19] However, the committee's recommendations were presented to Congress as a single bill based upon the integrated viewpoints of all the departments involved. Naturally, there was criticism of the bill. The congressional committees, as was perfectly proper, considered the supporting data on both sides of the question.

17 Edwin E. Witte, *Social Security in America* (Washington, 1937), p. v.

18 This was the case, however, only in connection with certain paid employees of the Committee on Economic Security. There was no such feeling among the permanent administrative officials on the cabinet committee or the Technical Board.

19 *Hearings before Senate Committee on Finance* (74th Congress, 1st session), on S. 1130; *Hearings before Committee on Ways and Means,* House of Representatives (74th Congress, 1st session), on H. R. 4120.

Careful reading of the staff reports and congressional hearings, supplemented by testimony of individuals connected with the committee, leads to the conclusion that the major contribution to the legislative proposals and the act as finally passed was made by the committee's staff of specialists and the interdepartmental Technical Board. The Technical Board "was given general direction of the studies and investigations to be undertaken by the Committee, and throughout the entire period in which the Committee's recommendations were formulated, functioned in closest cooperation with the Committee and its staff."[20] The executive staff of the cabinet committee digested and integrated a vast amount of technical information submitted as memoranda and reports. The final choice between alternative policies was made by the cabinet committee, subject to the personal scrutiny and approval of President Roosevelt. It cannot be doubted, however, that the discussions of the cabinet committee were immensely aided and made more fruitful by the factual information supplied by the Executive Director, his staff, and the officials of the Technical Board. There was disagreement within the cabinet group, down to the date that that last signature was affixed to the report. However, all the members felt that the success of the program depended to a large extent on the cabinet committee reaching unanimous agreement on a set of recommendations. President Roosevelt had set Christmas as the absolute deadline for the recommendations of the Committee on Economic Security. Two days before Christmas, the cabinet committee held a special meeting at which the Executive Director and the chairman of the Technical Board were present. This was a six-hour session, and was informal in the sense that no record was kept of the discussion. Agreement was reached on all essential points, and recommendations were submitted to the President on the following day.

On the whole, it can be said that the Committee on Economic Security is an example of the successful use of an interdepart-

20 Edwin E. Witte, *op. cit.*, p. iv.

mental committee to explore legislative proposals. The committee accomplished the three objectives implicit in its mandate. First, the problems of a social security program were explored in detail, and an attempt was made to think through the implications of alternative policies. To be sure, the committee's conclusions may not always have been the wisest possible. It may be that future developments will reveal the committee's decisions to have been wrong in certain aspects. Second, the varying viewpoints of governmental agencies engaged in welfare work were adjusted in the work of the executive staff and in the discussions of the cabinet committee and Technical Board. The genuineness and permanence of coordination here are indicated by the subsequent establishment of the Interdepartmental Committee on Health and Welfare, integrating the working policies of the welfare agencies under the Social Security Act. Third, the committee furnished a convenient focus for contact with Congress, and also for the general dissemination of information to the public.

The reasons for the committee's high degree of effectiveness have been suggested in the foregoing pages and need only be summarized here. In general, the committee exhibited an intelligent combination of organizational and personal factors. First, it built up a large staff, manned by reasonably competent personnel. Second, the technical groups worked hard. At least 137 memoranda, briefs, papers and similar reports were submitted to the Executive Director during the summer of 1934. Third, the Executive Director and his staff were tireless in reading reports, and in digesting and integrating them to frame a consistent program. Fourth, an extensive process of discussion, criticism and consultation was carried on. Fifth, control was always held in the small group organized around the Executive Director. Sixth, the Director himself was a man of competence, fitted by experience and temperament for leadership in the formulation of this program. Seventh, the committee's efforts were definitely concentrated upon the framing of legislative proposals, and a tentative bill was drafted.

The Committee on Economic Security may thus in many ways serve as a model for other interdepartmental groups exploring legislative proposals.[21] Its experience leaves no doubt of the usefulness of the interdepartmental committee for this type of activity. It happens that Dr. Witte was later called upon by the President's Committee on Administrative Management to study and report on the general problem of integrating the administration's legislative requests. His experience with the Committee on Economic Security is reflected in his recommendations. "All departments affected by the proposed legislation should be consulted and differences between them should be adjusted before introduction. Draftsmanship and questions of constitutionality should likewise be considered. At every stage the interests of the Government as a whole should be controlling, rather than those of any single department. . . . In this connection, use may well be made of interdepartmental committees on matters in which several departments are interested. Interdepartmental committees created ad hoc for the consideration of particular problems arising in connection with legislation seems much more likely than a single permanent agency to accomplish their purpose. Committees of this kind can be organized on the initiative of the President, of the Director of the Budget, or of the department initiating the proposed legislation." [22]

21 The success of the Committee on Economic Security cannot be considered typical of interdepartmental groups setting out to plan legislative proposals. As one outstanding contrast, the experience of the interdepartmental committee on Shipping Policy may be briefly described. This group was set up in 1934 to study, in cooperation with nationally known shipping authorities, broad questions relating to government shipping policy, merchant marine, and shipping code. It helped frame the Merchant Marine Act of 1935. The fact that it had submitted an inadequate report was shown when the new U. S. Maritime Authority (created by the Merchant Marine Act of 1935, in line with the recommendations of the Shipping Policy Committee) found itself with no clearly defined policy on which to operate. As a consequence, the whole question of shipping policy was reopened.

22 Edwin E. Witte, "The Preparation of Proposed Legislative Measures by Administrative Departments," in *Report and Special Studies*, President's Committee on Administrative Management (Washington, D. C., 1937), p. 376.

CHAPTER III

FUNCTIONAL COORDINATING COMMITTEES

WHAT characteristics distinguish the functional coordinating committee? How does it differ from the exploratory committee, which likewise coordinates and which also is concerned with the functional aspects of administration?[1] The distinction is between two stages in the development of administrative policy. Exploratory committees deal with policy in its initial stages, when long-range programs are being planned. The committees described in the present chapter are concerned with the problem of integrating the everyday operating policies of the agencies which administer the long-term program.

An important phase of this problem is the process of issuing administrative rules, regulations and orders. This is the rule-making power, which has been defined as "the legal authority of administrative officers or agencies of government to prescribe discretionary or interpretative rules and regulations of general applicability and legal effect."[2] It is clear from even a brief glance at administrative rule-making that the use of consultative techniques within the administration reflects directly

1 Throughout this study, the terms "functional" and "institutional" are used in the sense of W. F. Willoughby's definition. "Analysis of the duties or working activities of an administrative service shows that they fall into two clearly distinguishable classes: those which the service has to perform in order that it may exist and operate as an organization or institution, and those that it must perform in order to accomplish the ends for which it has been established and is being maintained. These two classes of activities may be designated as institutional and functional. . . . . The functional activities consist of the performance of the special or technical duties involved in carrying on the work for the performance of which the service is maintained." W. F. Willoughby, *Principles of Public Administration* (Brookings Institution, Washington, D. C., 1927), pp. 45-46.

2 James Hart, "The Exercise of Rule-Making Power," *Report and Special Studies*, President's Committee on Administrative Management (Washington, D. C., 1937), p. 319.

upon the conduct of the service relationships between government agent and citizen.[3] Devices which encourage a meeting of minds, such as the interdepartmental committee, help to give vitality, direction and continuity to departmental rule-making.

It is the task of the President to provide for clearance and coordination in the rule-making process throughout his administration.[4] To forestall or iron out conflicts between various agencies, and to keep administrative regulations in line with Presidential policies, consultative procedures are often useful. If coordination of administrative rule-making is to be effective, consultation must be employed while policies are " in the formative stage, before men's views have been hardened, or they have taken public positions on the questions involved, or conflicts have been aired in the press." [5] Moreover, the use of consultative techniques can be greatly encouraged by giving them the sanction of Presidential approval through an Executive Order.[6] An important interdepartmental committee will almost always receive recognition in an Executive Order.

3 There are two aspects, an external and an internal, to the rule-making process. " First, there are no fewer than 115 Federal agencies that, under 954 statutory provisions and 71 Executive orders and proclamations, issue rules and regulations that affect the public . . . Second, rule-making in the form of Executive orders is one of the principal techniques available to the President for the over-all management not only of departmental rule-making but also of the managerial operations of the Executive Branch." James Hart, *op. cit.*, p. 313.

4 The President derives his control over the rule-making process from three sources. First, his constitutional powers as commander-in-chief of the armed forces and as the nation's representative in foreign affairs, give him controlling authority within these specific fields. Second, Congress frequently delegates to the President or to his official subordinates power to fill in the interstices of a law by administrative regulations. Third, the President has a " general power of direction " implicit in his constitutional mandate to see that the laws are faithfully executed.

5 James Hart, *op. cit.*, p. 347.

6 The Executive Order is one of the principal instruments used for the exercise of the rule-making powers of the President. See James Hart, *op. cit.*, p. 320.

The present chapter will describe three significant attempts to bring the policies of separate agencies into line with each other or with a long-range Presidential program. The committees which have been selected for study are illustrative of three types of interdepartmental coordination of functional policy. The first case study will describe the group of interdepartmental committees concerned with the negotiation of foreign trade agreements. In this instance the activity is primarily entrusted to a single agency, the State Department. In the act of Congress which provided for the negotiation of trade agreements it was specified that, "Before concluding such agreements the President shall seek information and advice with respect thereto from the U. S. Tariff Commission, the Departments of State, Agriculture, and Commerce and from such other sources as he may deem appropriate."[7] Interdepartmental committees were set up to enable these agencies to work together in the new program, under the leadership of the State Department.

In the second case study, the Interdepartmental Committee on Health and Welfare, a number of agencies are separately responsible for different aspects of an important governmental activity. It happens that most of the federal agencies concerned with welfare work are located in different departments. For example, the Public Health Service is located in the Treasury Department, while the Division of Labor Standards is part of the Department of Labor. Both the Public Health Service and the Division of Labor Standards are attempting to help state governments control industrial health hazards. These two federal agencies work in unison by means of an interdepartmental subcommitte of the Committee on Health and Welfare. The subcommittee in effect directs the program. Integration is as effective, in this instance, as though the operating units were in the same department.

7 An Act to Amend the Tariff Act of 1930 (Public No. 316, 73rd Congress), approved June 12, 1934.

In the third case study, the Central Housing Committee, there is no single federal program in which all the operating agencies participate. Each functions under its separate legislative mandate. There is, of course, an obvious need for minimizing conflict among the housing agencies. The interdepartmental committee gives these agencies an opportunity to exchange information, compare viewpoints, and in general to keep informed about each others' policies.

THE INTERDEPARTMENTAL ORGANIZATION FOR NEGOTIATING TRADE AGREEMENTS [8]

The chain of events which brought into existence the present interdepartmental structure for integrating commercial policy and negotiating trade agreements began with the election of the 72nd Congress in 1930.[9] The victorious Democrats were prepared to denounce the Smoot-Hawley tariff and to adopt "a policy of mutual trade concessions" with foreign countries. Thus the Collier-Harrison bill, providing for the negotiation of

8 The trade agreements organization was selected as a case study because it is the most important program that has been undertaken by an interdepartmental committee of this type. Other committees which come within the classification are listed below; several of these have now disbanded.

Foreign Trade Zones Board.
Immigration Quota Committee.
Commission Created by the Grain Futures Act.
Regulatory Committee on Enforcement of the Pure Food and Drug Act.
Advisory Council for Government of the Virgin Islands.
Interdepartmental Committee on the Territory of Alaska.
Quetico-Superior Committee.
Migratory Bird Conservation Commission.
Committee to Cooperate with the Subsistence Homesteads Division.
Federal Committee on Apprentice Training.
Special Board for Public Works.
Interdepartmental Ice Patrol Board.
Advisory Council to the Director of the Emergency Conservation Work.
National Archives Council.
National Historical Publications Commission.
National Park Trust Fund Board.
Special Board for Industrial Recovery.

9 For research into the legislative background of the trade agreements committees I am indebted to Mr. W. J. Haggerty.

reciprocal trade agreements, was passed by Congress in May, 1932, but was vetoed by President Hoover.[10] In the Presidential campaign of 1932 Mr. Roosevelt indicated his intention of embarking on a program of bilateral tariff bargaining, and the administrative departments gradually began to orient their practices toward the new policy. Officials in the Departments of State and Commerce met together informally to plan an administrative structure for negotiating trade agreements. An arrangement closely resembling the present organization was outlined by an official of the Commerce Department early in 1933.

In October, 1933, President Roosevelt wrote to Secretary Hull, asking him to prepare suggestions for integrating the working policies of all governmental agencies concerned with the international commercial relations of the United States.[11] From this time forward, the State Department was the guiding force both in the planning and in the execution of the trade agreements program. The position of the State Department in the new program was the result of two considerations. In negotiations with foreign governments it seemed essential that a single agency should represent the United States. At the same time, the ramifications of the program demanded that all the agencies concerned with foreign trade be given some voice in the formulation of trade agreements. Secretary Hull presented to President Roosevelt a memorandum of recommendations based on these two principles. After conferring informally with officials of the State and Commerce departments, President Roosevelt sent the following letter to the heads of seven agencies.[12]

10 H. R. 662, 72nd Congress, 2nd session.

11 In addition to Secretary Hull, officials in several other departments were preparing suggestions for integration of commercial policy. Informal interdepartmental conferences were held, and it seems clear that the recommendations finally made to the President represented a consensus of opinion among the officials responsible for the conduct of international commercial relations.

12 The Departments of State, Treasury, Commerce, Agriculture, the Agricultural Adjustment Administration, the National Recovery Administration, and the U. S. Tariff Commission.

My dear Mr. Secretary:

It appears to me that the growing complexity of American commercial relations with foreign countries requires a new step in the systematization of the handling of these relations. This new step in systematization is dictated by two sets of circumstances:

(1) Under the Administration's program the numerous recovery departments are assigned powers or duties which directly touch upon trade relations with other countries. It is plain that the acts of each of the separate branches of the Government must be brought into a coherent policy system with the acts of all the rest.

(2) The changing policies of other governments and the changing methods of regulating international trade greatly complicate the Government's task of proper direction of American trade.

I therefore have decided to designate one officer in the Department of State to carry the primary responsibility of supervising the international commercial policy of this Government into a coherent whole. Hereafter may I ask that you give the necessary instructions in your department that before any acts are taken under legislation or otherwise which directly affect the export and import trade in this country, this official should be consulted concerning the action and his approval secured.

It is my idea that this official should be the chairman of an Executive Committee for the coordination of Commercial Policy and the negotiation of commercial treaties and trade agreements, and that in his decisions he would be very largely carrying out the judgment of the Committee. Upon this Committee your Department will be represented.

It is my further expectation that as this Committee develops its work, all subordinate interdepartmental committees engaged in the work of negotiating commercial treaties, the elaboration of trade agreements, etc., will report to the responsible official and through him to the government committee.

I also request that you instruct your Department that this official, as chairman of the coordinating committee, should be the regular channel of communication with all foreign governments on all policy matters affecting American export and import trade.

The arrangements contemplated in this order will be elaborated in further directions which will be transmitted later.

I have asked Mr. Phillips, Under Secretary of State, to undertake these duties as chairman of the coordinating committee until such time as a permanent selection is made. Therefore, pending further notice, he will be chairman pro tem.

(Signed) FRANKLIN D. ROOSEVELT.

November 11, 1933.

During the next several months the Executive Committee on Commercial Policy met at weekly intervals, supplementing its discussions by frequent conferences of smaller interdepartmental groups. The Committee's principal task during this period was the scrutiny and approval of proposals for enabling legislation for the trade agreements program.

The Trade Agreements Act was approved June 12, 1934.[13] It gave the President four important authorizations, which suggested the outlines of the new administrative structure.

1. To enter into foreign trade agreements with foreign governments or instrumentalities thereof.
2. To modify existing duties as are required or appropriate to carry out any foreign trade agreement that the President has entered into.
3. Before any agreement is concluded, public notice of intention to negotiate such an agreement shall be given in order that any interested person may have an opportunity to present his views to the President, or to such an agency as the President may designate, under such rules and regulations as the President may prescribe.
4. Before concluding such agreement the President shall seek information and advice with respect thereto from the U. S. Tariff Commission, the Departments of State, Agriculture and Commerce and from such other sources as he may deem appropriate.

State Department officials thereupon prepared a memorandum describing the proposed structure for negotiating trade agree-

13 Public No. 316, 73rd Congress (48 Stat. 943). The provisions of this act were extended by the act of March 1, 1937 (50 Stat. 24).

ments. On June 23, 1934, Secretary Hull sent the memorandum to the Secretary of Agriculture, Secretary of Commerce, Secretary of the Treasury, Chairman of the U. S. Tariff Commission, Special Adviser to the President on Foreign Trade, and the National Recovery Administrator, together with a letter saying: "If the main features of the plan meet with your approval I should appreciate your designating an officer or officers to act as the representative of your Department on the Committee on Foreign Trade Agreements described in the enclosed memorandum." This was the official launching of the trade agreements program.[14]

14 In this connection the relation of George N. Peek to the trade agreements program requires explanation. In September, 1933, Mr. Peek (then Administrator of AAA) submitted to the President certain memoranda outlining his views on foreign trade problems. On November 11, 1933, the President sent to Mr. Peek, *inter alia*, the letter establishing the temporary Executive Committee on Commercial Policy. On December 11, 1933, after repeated clashes with Secretary of Agriculture Wallace, Mr. Peek expressed his intention of resigning his post in AAA and opposing publicly the policies of Secretary Wallace. President Roosevelt, saying that he wanted to keep both Mr. Peek and Mr. Wallace in the administration, asked Mr. Peek to prepare some studies on foreign trade and suggested that he take the chairmanship of an informal interdepartmental committee to recommend new legislation on international commercial relations. Mr. Peek agreed, resigned from AAA, and during the next two months apparently worked along parallel lines with the Executive Committee on Commercial Policy. He also participated in the sessions of the Executive Committee.

On February 2, 1934, President Roosevelt created the First Export-Import Bank by Executive Order and on March 9 created the Second Export-Import Bank by Executive Order. In both cases, Mr. Peek was made President.

On March 23, 1934, Mr. Peek was made Special Adviser to the President on Foreign Trade, a post created specially for him by Executive Order 6651. The terms of the executive order were very broad but very vague. Mr. Peek interpreted them as a mandate based on some previous recommendations he had made to the President, and set about preparing a general audit of the United States' position in world trade from 1896 to 1934.

On March 27, the Executive Committee on Commercial Policy was reconstituted, by Executive Order 6656. Mr. Peek was made a member. From the beginning of the trade agreements program he consistently objected to the underlying policy of making tariff concessions in agreements with foreign countries. On June 30, 1934, Mr. Peek wrote to Louis M. Howe,

The accompanying chart will indicate how the agencies participating in the trade agreements program are connected by the structure of interdepartmental committees.[15]

The task of the Executive Committee on Commercial Policy is the consideration of general problems and the formulation of general policies for the trade agreements program as a whole.[16] It was hoped that this committee might frame an

saying that the trade agreements machinery was "adequate" but deploring the program in general and certain agreements in particular. As a member of the Executive Committee, Mr. Peek voted against nearly every agreement concluded.

On May 23 and August 30, 1934, and April 30, 1936, Mr. Peek presented three reports of his work as Special Adviser on Foreign Trade. On November 26, 1935, he resigned his position and left the administration.

It is significant that the Office of Special Adviser on Foreign Trade was never given any responsibility for operations, but always remained "advisory". This fact gives weight to the interpretation advanced by certain individuals in the trade agreements program: that the series of moves described above represented an attempt, first to "educate" Mr. Peek in the new policy of mutual trade concessions, and when that failed, to remove Mr. Peek, as tactfully as possible, first from the AAA and then from the administration; and while he remained in the administration, keeping him in such a position that his views could not hamper the progress of the trade agreements program.

The texts of most of the executive orders, letters and memoranda mentioned above have been reprinted in *Why Quit Our Own?* by George N. Peek and Samuel Crowther (D. Van Nostrand Co., New York City, 1936), pp. 140 ff.

15 This chart is reprinted from *America Must Act*, by Francis B. Sayre (World Affairs Pamphlets No. 13, World Peace Foundation, New York City, 1936), p. 52.

16 The Executive Committee on Commercial Policy was created by a letter of the President under date of November 11, 1933. In a Department of State Press Release of November 25, 1933 (p. 283), the creation of the Executive Committee was announced, with the following membership: William Phillips, Assistant Secretary of State, chairman pro tem; Walter J. Cummings, Treasury Department; John Dickinson, Assistant Secretary of Commerce; Willard L. Thorp, Department of Commerce; Rexford G. Tugwell, Assistant Secretary of Agriculture; William I. Westervelt, AAA; Oscar B. Ryder, NRA; Robert L. O'Brien, Chairman, U. S. Tariff Commission; and Thomas Walker Page, U. S. Tariff Commission. However the, active membership of the Committee from 1934 to 1936 included the following: Francis B. Sayre, Assistant Secretary of State, chairman; George N. Peek, Special Adviser to

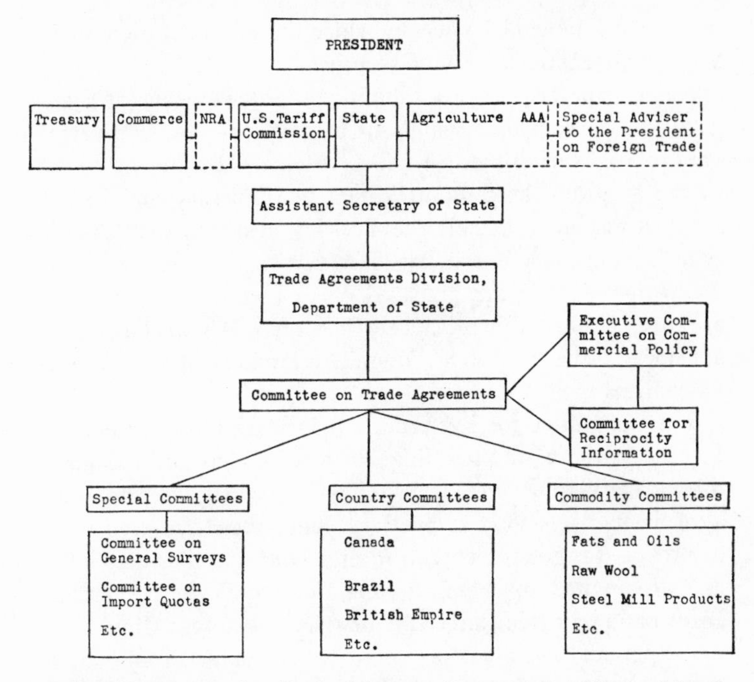

the President on Foreign Trade (alternate, Raymond C. Miller); John C. Dickinson, Assistant Secretary of Commerce, later replaced by Richard C. Patterson, Jr., Assistant Secretary of Commerce; Claudius T. Murchison, Bureau of Foreign and Domestic Commerce; Robert L. O'Brien, U. S. Tariff Commission; Thomas W. Page, U. S. Tariff Commission; Oscar B. Ryder, U. S. Tariff Commission; H. R. Tolley, Agricultural Adjustment Administration (alternate, Lynn R. Edminster); Henry F. Grady, Department of State; Henry A. Wallace, Secretary of Agriculture (alternate, L. A. Wheeler); George C. Haas, Treasury Department; H. D. Gresham, NRA.

The authority of the Executive Committee on Commercial Policy has been confirmed and extended by Executive Order 6656, March 27, 1934, and Executive Order 7260, December 31, 1935. In the latter, the "permanent membership" of the committee was defined, to consist of representatives from the Departments of State, Treasury, Agriculture, Commerce, the U. S. Tariff Commission, and the Agricultural Adjustment Administration. The present membership of the committee is as follows: Francis B. Sayre, Assistant Secretary of State, chairman; Wayne C. Taylor, Assistant Secretary of the Treasury; Henry A. Wallace, Secretary of Agriculture; Richard C. Patterson, Jr., Assistant Secretary of Commerce; Raymond B. Stevens, Chairman, U. S. Tariff Commission; Jesse W. Tapp, Assistant Administrator, AAA; Warren L. Pierson, President, Export-Import Bank.

integrated commercial policy by which the administration might be guided. Moreover, the Executive Committee votes on all agreements before they are submitted to the Secretary of State. The group is composed mainly of political officials, who devote only part of their time to trade agreements. In the early days of the program the committee met each Tuesday and Friday at 11 a. m., but gradually the Tuesday meetings were discontinued. Attendance has always been very regular and complete. No formal agenda are prepared, but materials for discussion are often circulated in advance of meetings. All official records and files of the Executive Committee are kept in the office of its chairman.

The Committee for Reciprocity Information was established for the purpose of providing business a convenient channel through which to present its views regarding specific trade agreements.[17] As soon as public announcement has been made of proposed negotiations with foreign countries, business interests are invited to submit to the Committee on Reciprocity Information written statements of their views regarding either the export or the import aspects of the proposed trade agree-

17 The Committee for Reciprocity Information was created by Executive Order 6750, June 27, 1934. In a State Department Press Release of July 3, 1934, the membership of this committee was announced as follows: Thomas Walker Page, U. S. Tariff Commission; Robert Frazer, American Consul General, Department of State; Leslie A. Wheeler, Division of Foreign Agricultural Service, Department of Agriculture; Henry Chalmers, Chief, Division of Foreign Tariffs, Department of Commerce; John Lee Coulter, Office of Special Adviser to the President on Foreign Trade; and H. D. Gresham, Acting Chief, Imports Division, NRA. However, the active membership of this committee between 1934 and 1936 included the following: Thomas Walker Page, U. S. Tariff Commission, chairman; E. M. Whitcomb, U. S. Tariff Commission, executive secretary; John Lee Coulter, Office, of Special Adviser to the President on Foreign Trade; L. E. Van Norman, Department of Commerce; Thomas Hughes, Department of State; Leslie A. Wheeler, Department of Agriculture; and James E. Burke, National Recovery Administration. The State Department's present policy precludes making public the names of the present members of the committee, but it may be assumed that most of the original members who are still in the Government service have remained active in the trade agreements program.

ment. Those who have submitted written statements but who desire to present further views orally may do so upon application. Hearings held before the committee are open to the public. Notice of intentions to negotiate, and also the regulations of the Committee on Reciprocity Information governing the manner of presenting views, are published in *Commerce Reports* of the Department of Commerce, and in *Press Releases* of the Department of State.[18] In order that interested persons may have ample opportunity to present their views, a period of at least six or seven weeks following the date of the public notice of intended negotiations is allowed for submitting written statements to the committee. Oral statements are usually received about one week later. All information received either orally or in writing by the Committee on Reciprocity Information is referred promptly to the Committee on Trade Agreements for consideration by the appropriate country committee.

The Trade Agreements Division of the Department of State serves as a central secretariat for the program. Under the direction of its Chief, Harry C. Hawkins, who is also chairman of the Trade Agreements Committee, the Trade Agreements Division takes the initiative in appointing subcommittees, assigning research, and checking up on progress. The Trade Agreements Division was originally set up as part of the office of Assistant Secretary of State Francis B. Sayre. Mr. Sayre is, under the Secretary of State, responsible for the leadership of conversations with foreign governments. He is also chairman of the Executive Committee on Commercial Policy. In 1935, the volume and importance of the work done by the Trade

18 These regulations were drawn together in the July 12 and September, 1934 numbers of *Treasury Decisions*, of the Treasury Department. The Committee on Reciprocity Information itself prepared a circular, "Suggestions as to Method and Character of Representations to the Committee on Reciprocity Information," which was mimeographed and made available to the general public in December, 1937. Another mimeographed circular, "Rules of Practice and Procedure of the Committee for Reciprocity Information, Adopted June 9, 1938," was prepared for the *Federal Register*.

Agreements Division led to its reorganization as a separate division of the State Department, with its own chief.[19]

The Committee on Trade Agreements is the central base of strategy for the negotiation of trade treaties.[20] As the nucleus of the interdepartmental organization, this group has a dual task. First, it reviews each proposed trade agreement, examining in detail the concessions recommended for inclusion in the new tariff schedules. Second, it considers all matters of operating policy. The Committee on Trade Agreements and the Executive Committee on Commercial Policy often cover the same ground. However, the vote taken by the Executive Committee on each trade agreement is merely a formality, while the scrutiny given to trade agreements by the Committee on Trade Agreements is detailed and complete, and the decisions of the latter group are decisive as to what concessions shall be included in the draft agreement. The members of the Committee on Trade Agreements are technical or professional people, permanent career men rather than political officials. Members of

19 This reorganization was accomplished by a departmental order of the Department of State, May 27, 1935.

20 The Trade Agreements Committee was established by the Executive Committee on Commercial Policy, June 22, 1934. Its creation was announced by letter of the Secretary of State, June 23, 1934. The original membership of the committee was as follows: Henry F. Grady, Department of State, chairman; Alvin H. Hansen, Department of State, vice-chairman; James H. Edwards, Office of Special Adviser to the President on Foreign Trade; Henry Chalmers, Department of Commerce; Louis Pasvolsky, Department of Commerce (alternate, Louis Domeratsky); Oscar B. Ryder, U. S. Tariff Commission (alternate, A. M. Fox); Lynn R. Edminster, Agricultural Adjustment Administration; Eli Frank, Jr., Treasury Department; Harry D. White, Treasury Department; Leslie A. Wheeler, Department of Agriculture; H. R. Gresham, National Recovery Administration.

When the Trade Agreements Division of the Department of State was organized in May, 1935, the new Chief of this Division, Harry C. Hawkins, was also made chairman of the Trade Agreements Committee. Since that time, the State Department has followed a policy of not making public the membership of the Trade Agreements Committee. It may be assumed, however, that most of the original members who are still in the Government service have remained active.

this group customarily devote their full time to the preparation of trade agreements, while many of the members of the Executive Committee on Commercial Policy consider the trade agreements program only one part of their activity in the national administration. In practice, the distinction between administrative problems and political problems as the concern respectively of the Committee on Trade Agreements and the Executive Committee largely disappears. The Committee on Trade Agreements does not attempt to frame a commercial policy for the country, and refers to the Executive Committee matters which are broadly political in nature. But the discussions of the Executive Committee are almost always based on facts supplied by the Committee on Trade Agreements or its subcommittees. Moreover, there is a good deal of interrelation of personnel between these two policy-framing committees. For example, when the Executive Committee on Commercial Policy created a subcommittee to study our trade relations with Japan, officials of the Committee on Trade Agreements served as members of the subcommittee.

The Committee on Trade Agreements operates through the three types of ad hoc subsidiary committees shown on the chart above. The first type is the special research committee, set up to examine and report upon a particular problem. A large number of such committees have been created. For example, a Committee on General Surveys was established by the Committee on Trade Agreements on June 28, 1934, for the purpose of planning and coordinating a number of factual studies on the basis of which the Committee on Trade Agreements might decide questions of general policy.[21] Another special research committee created by the Committee on Trade Agreements was

21 Members of this committee were:

Alvin H. Hansen, Department of State (chairman).
Charles F. Darlington, Office of the Special Adviser to the President.
A. M. Fox, U. S. Tariff Commission.

the Committee on Import Quotas.[22] This group was set up in the first place to study the subject of quotas and to formulate the policy of the Committee on Trade Agreements concerning quotas; later it was given the task of considering requests from foreign countries regarding their importations, and correspondingly of furnishing facts on which this country's demands might be based. The Committee on Import Quotas now participates in the drafting of each trade agreement, consulting with the country committees and submitting recommendations to the Committee on Trade Agreements.

The second type of subsidiary committee is the country committee. This is a small interdepartmental group created to carry on the detailed preliminary work of drafting the trade agreement. A country committee is created for each country with which the United States contemplates negotiations. The country committee is usually composed of five, and never more than nine members, including representatives from the Departments of State, Commerce, Agriculture, Treasury and the Tariff Commission. At first it was intended that the country committee would not only be a research group but would also conduct preliminary technical discussions with experts from the foreign country involved,[23] but it seems clear that the country committees as such have confined their work to the direction of research. Occasionally some members of the country committee will participate in the official welcome to the foreign representatives, and in a few cases a member of the country committee has been chosen to participate in negotiations, but this has by

22 Members of this committee were Oscar B. Ryder, U. S. Tariff Commission (chairman).
Henry Chalmers, Department of Commerce.
Lynn R. Edminster, AAA.
Henry F. Grady, State Department.
Frederick Livesey, State Department.
L. A. Wheeler, Department of Agriculture.

23 Plan of organization adopted by the Committee on Trade Agreements at its meeting of June 28, 1934, and approved by the Executive Committee on Commercial Policy, June 29, 1934.

no means been the rule. The identity of the individuals who serve on the country committees, and also those who conduct the actual negotiations, is kept secret by the State Department in order to safeguard the negotiators from pressure. Thirteen country committees were appointed by the Committee on Trade Agreements when the organization was first set up, and additional groups are created as necessity arises.

The third type of subsidiary committee is the commodity committee. These are small interdepartmental groups established by the Committee on Trade Agreements to study the import and export trade in special commodities. The State Department's policy of secrecy extends to the membership of the commodity committees. Through the commodity committees, the Committee on Trade Agreements has been furnished with general marketing analyses regarding fats and oils, raw wool, steel mill products, petroleum products, alcoholic liquors, dairy products, fruits and nuts, machinery, and textile products, *inter alia.*

How has the trade agreements structure integrated the policies of its constituent departments? It is possible to reply to this query only in general terms. The work of negotiating trade agreements is necessarily of a highly confidential nature. Secrecy is the rule all along the line. It is practically impossible to reconstruct the discussions of the two major policy-framing agencies, the Executive Committee on Commercial Policy and the Trade Agreements Committee. We can, however, trace some of the issues which were discussed by the Executive Committee. We can also indicate the nature of the work of the Committee on Trade Agreements by describing some of the problems involved in the process of tariff bargaining.

The main reason for using an interdepartmental committee to discuss broad questions of commercial policy is to maintain that policy in a balance between agricultural and commercial interests in the first place, and between importing and exporting interests in the second place. When tariff hearings were held by congressional committees, agricultural interests were usually subordinated to industrial interests.[24] With the introduction of a new procedure, an opportunity arose for integrating commercial policy with agricultural policy, foreign commercial relations with domestic programs. In practice this meant simply that the presence of the Secretary of Agriculture on the Executive Committee on Commercial Policy tended to insure consideration of the farmer's particular interests. There can be no doubt that the presence of this official on the Executive Committee has resulted in improved integration of agricultural and commercial factors in American foreign policy. This does not mean that Secretary Wallace has in any way taken a narrowly partisan stand for agricultural interests. At no time has he done this. He is, rather, the spokesman for certain viewpoints and interests which cannot be left out of account in framing a commercial policy truly comprehensive and genuinely in the public interest.

The Executive Committee has also been aware of the implications of our commercial policy for general foreign policy. Thus it set up a standing subcommittee to study our trade relations with Japan. It cannot be doubted that the information gathered by the subcommittee on Japan has been used by the State Department in advising the President and congressional leaders on such problems as the Far Eastern crisis and Philippine independence. The interesting question, however, is whether the discussions of the Executive Committee on Commercial Policy have had any effect on the handling of these problems by the governmental agencies concerned. Organized farm groups largely favor Philippine independence.[25] The State Department, however, does not. The War and Navy departments too would prefer to retain control of the Islands.[26] Here,

24 See Henry A. Wallace, *America Must Choose* (World Affairs Pamphlet No. 3, Foreign Policy Association, New York City, 1934), pp. 10 *et seq.*

25 See Grayson L. Kirk, *Philippine Independence* (Farrar and Rinehart, New York, 1936), Chapter IV.

26 See *Hearings before the Senate Committee on Military Affairs*, 66th Congress, 1st session (1919), pp. 211, 623-24, 964-65.

then, are points of conflict between departmental viewpoints which concern vital national problems, and which are consequently the logical subjects for discussion by a committee seeking to integrate the administration's commercial policy.

The State Department feels that the Executive Committee has been quite successful in its primary objective. " Matters affecting the commercial relations of the United States with foreign countries which come within the jurisdiction of any member department or other agencies are referred to the Committee before action is taken. By thus centralizing in the hands of one agency supervision of all governmental action affecting export and import trade, coordination of commercial policy between the various departments and agencies is facilitated." [27] There have been disagreements and failures, of course. It is known that at least on one occasion the Secretary of Agriculture ignored a decision of the Committee against dumping of agricultural surpluses. On the whole, however, the Executive Committee has achieved a greater degree of integration of the agencies involved than has ever before been the case. Quantitatively, the degree of coordination of routine decisions has been satisfactory. When matters of vital departmental policy have been touched, coordinating efforts have not always been successful. Larger issues of foreign policy have certainly been discussed, but the discussions have had no perceptible effect on governmental action.

The Committee on Trade Agreements, together with the Trade Agreements Division and the numerous subsidiary committees, must be given credit for very substantial achievements. The general objectives of the interdepartmental organization are, " The compilation of all pertinent data, the consideration of all significant factors, the full availability of expert advice, and the receipt of the views of business with respect to pro-

27 U. S. State Department, *The Department of State of the United States* (Washington, D. C., rev. to June, 1936), pp. 42-43. See also " How Trade Agreements are Made," by Francis B. Sayre, *Foreign Affairs*, April, 1938.

posed trade agreement negotiations." [28] The discussions of the Committee on Trade Agreements, ideally considered, have been an attempt to study the American economy in the perspective of its international aspects, analyzing it in detail with reference to individual commodities and the special problems of agriculture and labor. Under the active leadership of the Committee on Trade Agreements, the efforts of the Trade Agreements Division, the Committee on Reciprocity Information, and the subsidiary research committees have been directed toward this general objective. Let us first review some of the problems which the Committee on Trade Agreements has discussed, and then trace the process of negotiating a typical trade agreement.

One set of problems discussed by the Committee on Trade Agreements concern the export trade. The committee set out to study competitive conditions in world markets, so that it might give intelligent consideration to the probable effects of changes in American tariffs on the import restrictions of foreign countries. Studies were also made at the outset of the problems of American industries whose existence depends primarily on world markets—in short, the export industries.[29] The Committee on Trade Agreements set up research subcommittees to study and report upon such subjects as quotas, exchange control, and similar import restrictions; the treatment accorded American commerce in the operation of such restrictions; the existence of American branch factories in foreign countries, and the allocation of production between the domestic and the foreign units. The representation of several federal agencies on these research subcommittees on the one hand assured coverage of all the data which these agencies possess,

28 "Foreign Trade Agreements", mimeographed circular, U. S. State Department.

29 See *Recommendations of the Committee on Commercial Policy*, Foreign Policy Committee Reports No. 3 (Foreign Policy Association and World Peace Foundation, New York City, March, 1934), p. 4.

and on the other hand provided for consideration of varied points of view.

A second set of problems are those concerned with specific negotiations. The preliminary work for a proposed trade agreement requires examination of virtually every item exchanged between the United States and the country concerned. It is particularly important to know what percentage of our imports of any commodity on which a concession is requested is supplied by the negotiating country. If that country is not the principal or at least an important supplier of the commodity in question, it generally follows that a concession on that product will be of greater value if reserved for tariff bargaining with a country which is the chief or an important source.[30] For example, the United States is a net importer of beef and cattle, and is a natural market for Canada. In negotiating the trade agreements with Canada, therefore, the prime importance of cattle in Canadian-American trade, and the vital interests of the prairie provinces in cattle raising, made a tariff concession on live cattle imported into the United States a *sine qua non* of successful negotiation. In all such cases, extensive research is essential to discover and interpret the true situation.

A third set of problems concerns the effect of tariff reductions on government revenues. Here, the representation of the Treasury Department on the interdepartmental committee is obviously required. In the case of certain imported commodities for which the domestic demand is relatively inelastic and on which the existing duty is especially productive of government revenues, the loss in revenue that would result from a reduction in the duty might be out of proportion to the expected increase in trade.

As the first step in negotiating a trade agreement, the Secretary of State publishes notices of intentions to negotiate in

30 For an elaboration of the "principal supplier" idea, see Francis B. Sayre, *America Must Act*. For a statement of the opposing viewpoint, see George N. Peek, *Why Quit Our Own?* (D. Van Nostrand Co., New York City, 1936), pp. 253 ff.

Press Releases of the Department of State, the weekly *Treasury Decisions,* and *Commerce Reports.* A statement is also issued to the press. This procedure is fixed by Executive Order.[31] The Committee for Reciprocity Information then announces that it will receive the views of persons interested in the pending negotiations. "At the time public notice is given of intention to negotiate a trade agreement, the general nature of the trade between the United States and the country concerned is indicated by tables of statistics in regard to the principal commodities entering into the trade. Additional statistical information in regard to any article of import or export may be obtained upon request from the Division of Foreign Trade Statistics or the District Offices of the Department of Commerce. Other information in regard to trade or tariff matters may be obtained from the Department of Commerce or the Tariff Commission. It seems reasonable, therefore, to assume that American producers, importers, exporters, and other interested persons would know whether the country with which a trade agreement is to be negotiated is of any consequence as a source of supply, or as a market for, the product or products in which they are interested, and that they would also know the factors affecting the trade in such products.[32]

Typical of the way in which interests make their wishes articulate was the experience of the Committee on Reciprocity Information in connection with the trade agreement with Great Britain. Open hearings were held from March 14 to March 21, 1938. Violent opposition to the negotiations came from the textile and shoe industries of New England. Spokesmen for industrial, civic, and labor organizations denounced the agreement as not being founded on comprehensive cost of production statistics.

The president of the Cotton Textile Institute, Dr. Claudius T. Murchison, argued that the industry's price structure had

31 Executive Order No. 6750, June 27, 1934.

32 "Foreign Trade Agreements," mimeographed circular, U. S. Department of State.

already crumbled and that its wage structure would be destroyed by reduction of tariffs. He even went so far as to argue that the whole policy of tariff bargaining was unsound. "We may lose balance in our economic structure, and increase our dependence upon foreign markets. We may face costly and painful transfer of workers from occupations and industries and areas to which they are adjusted into new modes of life which rest precariously upon the fortunes of foreign trade." [33] The National Association of Cotton Manufacturers, the New Bedford Cotton Manufacturers Association, the Cotton Thread Institute, Textiles, Inc., and the Farmville Oil and Fertilizer Company also presented their views to the Committee.

Fifteen Republican Congressmen from New England reiterated the need for basing trade agreements on cost of production studies.[34] One Massachusetts Representative appeared in person before the Committee, asking rate increases instead of reductions, on shoes, wool, cotton textiles, paper products, textile machinery, and electrical products. One of the most interesting incidents was the appearance of Representative Allen of Pennsylvania to warn against lowering tariffs on products of the monopolistically controlled aluminum industry. He stated that the Aluminum Company of America would be forced to reduce its operations if tariff rates were lowered. Representative Pierce of Oregon protested against lowered rates on woolen and worsted goods. Representative Parsons of Illinois asked for protection of the fluorspar industry, and Representative Case of South Dakota for tariffs on manganese and feldspar.

33 *New York Times*, March 22, 1938, p. 4. The appearance of Dr. Murchison in opposition to the negotiations is of particular interest, inasmuch as he was for some time chief of the Bureau of Foreign and Domestic Commerce, and one of the original appointees to the Executive Committee on Commercial Policy in 1933.

34 See *New York Times*, March 15, 1938, pp. 1 and 4. In this instance Secretary Hull took the unusual step of replying with a contrary statement. Ordinarily the views presented to the Committee on Reciprocity Information are transmitted to the Committee on Trade Agreements without argument.

All information received by the Committee for Reciprocity Information is referred at once to the appropriate country committee. It is the duty of the country committee to assemble and analyze all available pertinent data, from both official and private sources, including the information and also including the data compiled by the commodity committees. Information on foreign trade is gathered by approximately 50 federal agencies. The vast files of the Tariff Commission and its 150 staff economists are the principal sources of information on commodities. The membership of the country committee and commodity committees invariably includes one man from the Tariff Commission who goes to the files and starts a staff of economists collecting and interpreting data. Numerous charts and tables are prepared, which ultimately develop into a schedule of concessions which this country may grant. Similarly, a schedule of concessions to be requested by this country is drawn up on the basis of data and recommendations submitted to the country committee by the Department of Commerce.

The final report of the country committee has three colunms: the present status of tariff schedules in our trade with the country concerned, suggested revisions of tariff schedules, and remarks. In final form, this report represents a consensus of the opinions of all the departments involved in the trade agreements program. The country committee goes over every item of the report in its meetings. Sometimes there is a clash between departmental viewpoints. Facts may have been interpreted differently by the Tariff Commission and the Department of Commerce; the representative of the latter agency may point out certain weaknesses in the memoranda supplied by the former, and the memoranda will thereupon be revised. The country committee considers political as well as economic factors in preparing its report. For example, in planning for tariff bargaining with Canada, the Department of Agriculture pointed out that 1936 was an exceptionally favorable time to offer concessions on live cattle imported into the United States. The amount of cattle slaughter in the United States would be smaller in the immediate future as a result of the 1936 drought. In other words, additional supplies would come from Canada regardless of tariffs, and the United States might as well seek reciprocal concessions (and also build up Canadian good will) in exchange for increased imports of cattle.

The final recommendations of the country committee are submitted to the Committee on Trade Agreements in the form of a report consisting usually of several volumes. The Committee on Trade Agreements goes over every item of the recommendations and supporting data, and a long discussion ensues before the schedules are approved. The Committee on Trade Agreements is greatly aided in this part of its work by the fact that one or more of its members always serve on the country committee and usually as chairman. When the Committee on Trade Agreements has approved the report, it is sent to the Executive Committee on Commercial Policy for a vote of approval which is largely a formality. The report is also scrutinized by the Secretary of State and the Assistant Secretary of State in charge of negotiations. Thereafter, the chairman of the country committee, or sometimes the chairman of the Committee on Trade Agreements, or possibly Mr. Sayre, takes the schedule of proposals to the President. Customarily, President Roosevelt has given each report about an hour's consideration. He has occasionally altered the committee's recommendations, always on political rather than economic grounds. Members of the Committee on Trade Agreements testify that President Roosevelt has an extraordinary capacity for singling out of the mass of recommendations precisely those items that may stimulate political opposition from sectional or occupational groups.

After receiving Presidential sanction, the recommendations are used by the American negotiators as a guide in the conversations with representatives of the foreign country concerned. At first the foreign representatives deal with a group, but in the end negotiations are carried on by a single individual. Questions arising in the course of negotiations may be referred to the country committee for consideration and recommendation, and members of such committees may be called upon to sit in on the negotiations to advise the American representatives. The ultimately decisive factors are not always economic, but neither are they narrowly partisan or the dictates of pressure groups. To cite the Canadian agreement once more, a quota was finally fixed for importation of Canadian cattle at the reduced tariff rate. Establishment of a quota served notice that Canada could not expect unlimited entry of cattle at the lower duty, and thus allayed the alarm of American producers. It was also felt that fixing a quota might appear more consistent with our domestic program of production control, though this was not actually a factor at the time.[35]

From the administrative viewpoint it seems clear that the trade agreements organization has been almost completely successful. As a piece of administrative machinery for the coordination of policy, the structure of interdepartmental committees has been effective both in the discussion of general problems and the conduct of an important program. At least three factors have contributed significantly to the success of the interdepartmental machinery.

The establishment of the trade agreements program firmly on a technical basis has been of considerable importance. It means that the members of the committees are continually working with concrete situations. They do not try to coordinate policy in the abstract. They try, rather, to adjust specific conflicts by means of discussion and compromise. There is a vast amount of research and fact-finding involved. Apparently there is nothing quite so helpful as facts in bringing about attitudes of reasonableness and cooperation, and in breaking down rigidly departmental viewpoints.

35 For a discussion of the economic rather than the administrative achievements of the trade agreements organization, see "1937-38 Results under the Trade Agreement Program," by Henry Chalmers, *Commerce Reports* (Bureau of Foreign and Domestic Commerce, U. S. Department of Commerce), August 13, 1938.

The quality of the personnel engaged in the trade agreements program has been uniformly high, and personnel problems have been skillfully handled. Here, as throughout the case study, stress must be laid on the contribution of those men who, as the original members of the committees, designed the machinery and set it in motion. About a dozen individuals who gravitated toward each other in the early days have more or less consciously been the driving force of the organization. Four of the individuals in this inner circle are officials from the State Department, three from Commerce, two from the Tariff Commission, two from Agriculture, and one from the Treasury Department.[36] Naturally, the group has fluctuated somewhat in size and membership from year to year. Probably an energizing nucleus of this sort is an essential feature of coordination in large-scale operations. In addition, however, the trade agreements program has benefitted greatly by the use of technicians at all levels of the organization. The personnel of the Committee on Trade Agreements is highly professionalized. Members of the subsidiary committees are permanent career officials, for the most part, and such men work well together. Moreover, the excellent practice of overlapping the personnel of committees has made possible intelligent and well-informed discussion even in large groups like the Committee on Trade Agreements. Members of the Committee on Trade Agreements have been able, by serving on many subcommittees, to become specialists in varied aspects of trade agreements work and at the same time to view their specialties in the perspective of the program as a whole.

The fact that leadership of the program was fixed in a single agency, the Department of State, contributed to the success of the program in several ways. Leadership by a single agency is probably essential to the achievement of stability in any inter-

36 It is interesting to note that the original group included one department head, one Tariff Commissioner, and one assistant secretary; the rest of the members were technical and professional men of the rank of bureau chief or below.

departmental program of considerable magnitude. The role of Assistant Secretary of State Francis B. Sayre, as chairman of the Executive Committee on Commercial Policy and chief of the program as a whole, has been perfectly complemented by the work of Henry F. Grady and later Harry C. Hawkins as chairman of the Committee on Trade Agreements. State Department officials have also held the chairmanship in practically all the subsidiary committees. The Trade Agreements Division of the State Department has provided a convenient focus for research. Moreover, public relations have been completely centralized in the State Department. Consequently, it has been possible to conduct research and negotiations in complete privacy until the time seemed appropriate for a public announcement. Thus the individual has constantly been subordinated to the program. Conflicts have never been aired in the press. There has been no opportunity for personal rivalries to develop.

The basing of the trade agreements program on a vast accumulation of technical data, the skilful use of competent personnel, and the concentration of leadership in a single agency, have created an atmosphere highly conducive to consultation. The structure of interdepartmental committees has developed into an organization which has taken full advantage of these favorable circumstances.

Interdepartmental Committee on Health and Welfare [37]

Since the World War, the need for some sort of Department of Public Welfare has been frequently discussed and its need generally assumed, though its exact content has been a subject of controversy. The welfare activities of the government, such as public health services, education, protection of industrial labor standards, and more recently federal relief and public

37 The Interdepartmental Committee on Health and Welfare was selected for presentation as a case study chiefly because it has achieved considerable success in coordination, but partly also because of the importance and current

works, are conducted by agencies scattered through four federal departments: Treasury, Interior, Agriculture, and Labor.[38] Occasionally, attempts have been made to bring the policies of these agencies into line with each other. An Act of Congress passed in 1930 provided for coordination of federal public health activities.[39] By the same measure the Surgeon General was empowered to detail personnel from the Public Health Service to educational and research institutions for special studies and to extend the facilities of the Service to health officials and scientists engaged in research. The law also contemplated draw-

interest of the field of activity in which it operates. Other committees falling within the same classification as the Health and Welfare Committee are as follows:

Interdepartmental Committee on Civil International Aviation.
Pan-American Commercial Conference Committee.
Drought Committee of 1934.
Drought Committee of 1936.
Puerto Rican Hurricane Relief Committee.
Federal Bureau of Hospitalization.
Deposit Liquidation Board.
Joint Merchant Vessel Board.
Interdepartmental Committee on Airports of Entry.
Patents and Designs Board.
Aeronautical Board.
U. S. Council of National Defense.
Joint Board, Army and Navy.
The Codification Board (for Federal Register).
Arlington Memorial Amphitheater Commission.
Federal Board of Surveys and Maps.
Commodity Credit Corporation.
Export-Import Bank of Washington.
Advisory Committee on Allotments.
Public Health Board.

38 And, of course, the Social Security Board after 1935.

39 Act of April 9, 1930 (46 Stat. 150). "On request of the head of any executive department or establishment that is carrying on public health work, the Secretary of the Treasury may detail officers or employees of the Public Health Service to cooperate. He is also authorized to establish additional divisions in the Hygienic Laboratory to aid in solving all public health problems and to supply facilities for coordinating research by public health officials and other scientists."

ing outside experts into the general scheme by sanctioning the appointment of a National Advisory Health Council. This was coordination of a sort, but it did not solve the problem of integrating the policies of the departments concerned.

With the enactment of the Social Security Law in 1935, the need for concerted formulation of policy became imperative, particularly in the fields of industrial hygiene and public health nursing where the law provided for financial aid to local units cooperating with the federal authorities. Accordingly, an Interdepartmental Committee on Health and Welfare was set up by letter of President Roosevelt to the Secretaries of the Treasury, Interior, Agriculture and Labor.[40] The President said: " I am asking this Committee to include within the scope of its work not only health activities, but closely related welfare activities as well. As its immediate task I am instructing this Committee to assume responsibility for the appointment of a special committee to be composed of physicians and other technically trained persons within the government service to study and make recommendations concerning specific aspects of the Government's health activities. I am confident that this procedure will facilitate the consummation of a series of appropriate cooperative agreements between the various departments of the government. I am also hopeful that in this way we can eventually bring about a complete coordination of the government's activities in the health field." The letter named as members of the new committee Josephine Roche, Assistant Secretary of the Treasury, chairman, Oscar L. Chapman, Assistant Secretary of the Interior, M. L. Wilson, Assistant Secretary of Agriculture, and Arthur J. Altmeyer, Second Assistant Secretary of Labor. Shortly after the Social Security Board was organized, provision was made for including one of its members on the Committee on Health and Welfare.

The Committees uses an executive staff consisting of a part-time executive secretary, a full-time administrative assistant,

40 August 15, 1935.

and a full-time stenographer. This assistance is furnished by the departments on a contributory basis, since the Committee has no funds of its own. The task of the staff is to collect data on the basis of which the Committee's cooperative agreements are framed. To this end, individuals have been appointed to the staff by each of the agencies represented on the Committee.[41] Each of these staff members compiles data listing the authorization, functions and activities of his division which are related to health and welfare, together with a brief description of each activity and the details of its relationships with other divisions and agencies, federal, state and local. The Committee staff prescribes the form in which this information shall be collected, and uses it to prepare summaries for the Committee's use.

Three permanent subcommittees have been established. One is in the nursing field, with representatives from the Labor Department and the Public Health Service of the Treasury Department. A second is the subcommittee on industrial hygiene, involving the Division of Labor Standards and the Public Health Service. The third deals with food research and nutrition, with representatives from the Public Health Service, the Commerce Department, the Agriculture Department, and certain universities.

The Committee on Health and Welfare meets infrequently. It functions as a board of review for the work of the subcommittees and the staff, and consequently meets only when interdepartmental negotiations have reached the point of formal agreement. Both program and machinery are very direct and simple.

Four of the formal cooperative agreements to which President Roosevelt alluded in his authorization have been concluded through the efforts of the Committee. The first of these relates to the public health nursing services of the Children's Bureau and the Public Health Service, and was framed by the sub-

41 Six representatives from the Department of Agriculture, four from Interior, four from Labor, two from WPA, and six from the Treasury.

committee appointed to deal with this field.[42] The subcommittee met in 1935 and adopted a statement of objectives. Its principal aim was described as the unification of administrative policies and the avoidance of duplication in nursing activity. Thereafter the group held a series of meetings and constructed a formal cooperative agreement, providing that all public health nursing services under federal auspices are to be so organized that general policies will be agreed upon at joint conferences of all federal agencies concerned. All regional consultation services, regardless of departmental organization, will be correlated by joint conferences, both in Washington and in the field. Conflicting recommendations regarding qualifications of nursing personnel are avoided by agreement upon uniform standards. When this agreement has been drawn up it was considered at a meeting of the Committee on Health and Welfare and was signed by the members. It has since served as the basis for the activity of the Children's Bureau and the Public Health Service in the field of public health nursing.

The second agreement sets up a functional division of activities between the Public Health Service and the Department of Labor, in the field of industrial hygiene. It was framed by the subcommittee on industrial hygiene, and the procedure followed was identical with that in the first case described.[43] The agreement assigns to the Public Health Service investigations of a medical and engineering nature to measure existing health

42 The personnel of this subcommittee is as follows: Miss Naomi Deutsch, Director Public Health Nursing Service, Department of Labor; Dr. Martha Eliot, Assistant Chief, Children's Bureau, Department of Labor; Dr. G. E. Waller, Assistant Surgeon General, Public Health Service, Treasury Department, and Miss Pearl MacIver, Associate Public Health Nursing Analyst, Public Health Service, Treasury Department.

43 The personnel of this subcommittee is as follows: Mr. Verne A. Zimmer, Division of Labor Standards, Department of Labor; Mrs. Clara M. Beyer, and Dr. R. R. Jones from the same bureau; Assistant Surgeon General L. R. Thompson, Public Health Service, Treasury Department, and Assistant Surgeon General C. E. Waller from the same agency; and Dr. R. R. Sayers, Surgeon in charge of the Office of Industrial Hygiene and Sanitation, Public Health Service, Treasury Department.

hazards and to determine procedures for control. It delegates to the Department of Labor the gathering and distribution of information on working conditions, accidents and wages. The agreement also recommends that state health departments be responsible for such activities as compilation of information on mortality in the working population, epidemiological studies of illness, technical service and advice, and the promotion of state legislation where it is necessary to the improvement of industrial health conditions. State labor departments are urged to assume responsibility for the adoption and enforcement of rules and regulations essential in the control of existing and potential health hazards, and for the promotion of such state legislation as is necessary to control those hazards.

The Subcommittee on Food Research and Nutrition coordinates the activity of three agencies, the Department of Commerce, the Department of Agriculture, and the Public Health Service of the Treasury Department, by means of a working arrangement which has never been written into a formal agreement but which appears to be completely satisfactory in practice. The arrangement grew out of a conference called by Secretary Roper on December 11, 1935, to consider a joint resolution which proposed to create a National Food Research Commission with an appropriation of $500,000.[44] This resolution had been sponsored by Dr. William Weston, chemist of the State of South Carolina, and had the approval of the American Medical Association. The Department of Commerce became interested in it because of certain potentialities which it offered in connection with the Bureau of Fisheries' Work, and Secretary Roper included in his conference representatives of the Public Health Service and the Department of Agriculture. The conference referred the whole matter to the Interdepartmental Committee on Health and Welfare. It was at this time that the technical subcommittee was appointed.[45] The subcom-

44 H. J. Res. 248 (74th Congress, 1st session).

45 With the following membership:

The Surgeon General of the Public Health Service, represented by As-

mittee met on January 13, 1936, and recommended that instead of the passage of the joint resolution, a permanent technical subcommittee be established to handle the activities contemplated. This was done, and the subcommittee (its membership unchanged) now meets with the technical staffs of federal agencies concerned with nutrition problems, assists with technical advice, and helps in making the results of research available to the medical profession and to the public.

The fourth cooperative agreement was put into effect by an exchange of letters between Secretary of the Treasury Henry B. Morgenthau, and Resettlement Administrator Rexford G. Tugwell. This arrangement, which now applies to the Farm Security Administration, concerns the furnishing of medical aid in the activity of the Resettlement Administration. A division of labor is the primary objective. The Public Health Service has assigned a full-time officer to head the work, with scientific and clerical assistance being supplied by Resettlement Administration, now the Farm Security Administration. The latter agency provides medical care for its beneficiaries, and has arranged to support and press for funds and authority necessary to augment the local health services of any community where special health problems are likely to result from its operations. Like the others, this agreement was first framed by representatives of the two agencies involved and was then approved by the Interdepartmental Committee on Health and Welfare.

The obvious criterion of this committee's success is the degree to which its formal cooperative agreements have actually been made the basis of action within the departments signing

sistant Surgeon General L. R. Thompson, the Secretary of Commerce, represented by Charles E. Jackson, of the Bureau of Fisheries, and Dr. John R. Manning, representative of the Fisheries Advisory Commission, the Secretary of Agriculture, represented by Dr. H. G. Knight and Dr. E. R. Blanck, Dr. William Weston, Chemist of the State of South Carolina, Passed Assistant Surgeon W. H. Sebrell, National Institute of Health, Professor E. V. McCollum, School of Hygiene, John Hopkins University, Professor H. C. Sherman, Department of Chemistry, Columbia University, and Dr. Harry Steenbock, University of Wisconsin.

the agreement. Most of these agreements have now been in force for well over a year, and as yet there has been no evidence either of abrogation or neglect. Officials throughout the Administration have no criticism but only praise for this experiment in coordination. The Committee was given a new grant of authority by Executive Order, on October 27, 1936, suggesting that it now has a more firmly established status.[46] Recent proposals for a Department of Public Welfare assume that such an organization might well be built on the foundation of interdepartmental relationships which this committee has built up. A Department of Public Welfare is generally favored by the personnel of the welfare agencies and the interdepartmental committee. Officials emphasize, however, that the activities of the committee would be continued in any case, for the purpose of tying into the new department the loose ends necessarily left by any reorganization, however sweeping.

Probably the immediate cause of the high degree of success which the Committee on Health and Welfare has achieved is the situation which was created by the Social Security Act. The need for coordination had always been present, even recognized, but sheer inertia and the weight of tradition long blocked its accomplishment. When the Social Security Act offered financial grants for health and welfare work in the states, the will toward coordination received the fresh impetus it needed.

A second major factor was the quality of the personnel in the central committee. Assistant Secretary of the Treasury Josephine Roche, as chairman, in particular contributed a driving energy, combined with a real and well-informed interest in public health services, without which the committee might never have been formed or have been so effective.[47] It is also significant that the members of the central committee were people

46 Executive Order No. 7481, October 27, 1936.

47 Miss Roche resigned her position as Assistant Secretary of the Treasury on September 14, 1937, to return to private life. However, at the request of President Roosevelt, Miss Roche has continued to be chairman of the Interdepartmental Committee on Health and Welfare.

of broad humanitarian instincts. Although their experience in public administration was slight, their " big brother " sense of responsibility was strong. In particular, Mr. Chapman and Mr. Wilson were not heavily burdened with administrative duties in their respective departments, a situation in accord with their own preferences. Mr. Chapman was virtually excluded from active responsibility in the Interior Department, and was consequently free to cultivate outside contacts. Mr. Wilson, having concluded his experience with Subsistence Homesteads, was practically a free lance, without much routine work to do in the Department of Agriculture.

Third, the committee was intelligently organized for its task. The technique of framing interdepartmental agreements was particularly fortunate. It concentrated the consultative process on fairly narrow, specific problems, and forced the use of specialists. Under such circumstances, once an agreement was adopted it was certain of enforcement, since the subcommittees which did the actual drafting were composed of the officials who later put the policies into effect.

Central Housing Committee [48]

Federal administrative agencies have been interested in housing problems for at least two decades. Such agencies as the Bureau of Home Economics, Bureau of Standards, Bureau of Yards and Docks, and construction divisions of the Veterans' Administration and the War Department, the National Park Service, and others have been contributing in various ways to the solution of housing problems ever since the World War period. Prior to 1933, however, the federal government's inter-

48 The Central Housing Committee was chosen for presentation as a case study partly because of the completeness of its records, partly also because of the importance and current interest of the activity with which it is concerned. Other committees of the same type are:

Industrial Emergency Committee.
Power Policy Committee of 1936.
Loan Committee.
Special Committee on Government Borrowing.

est in housing was largely confined to research. There was no direct federal construction except that which was found necessary at the time of the war, including the type of housing construction carried on near shipyards, munitions centers, and the like. Nor was there any serious promotion by the federal government of private construction or financing. This situation changed with the passage of the National Industrial Recovery Act. Between 1933 and 1935, there were in operation ten new federal agencies which dealt with housing as one of their major activities.

The aims and methods of these agencies diverged widely. The Farm Credit Administration sought to provide a cooperative credit system for agriculture, and also to make loans for the construction and improvement of farm houses. The Federal Home Loan Bank Board, with its subsidiary divisions and the Home Owners Loan Corporation,[49] operates today in the field of home mortgage finance, to encourage and assist private capital in increasing the volume of long-term home mortgage credit. The Federal Housing Administration issues long-term amortizing mortgages on homes, by means of a mutual mortgage insurance fund operated by the Administrator, who is authorized to insure first-mortgage loans made by approved lending institutions. The Housing Division of the Public Works Administration (now merged in the U. S. Housing Authority) engaged in direct construction and operation, from beginning to end, of low-rent housing projects. The Resettlement Administration, now absorbed into the Farm Security Administration of the Department of Agriculture, constructed homestead settlements intended to provide full or part-time farming for families on worn-out land, in cut-over areas or exhausted mining districts. This agency also constructed three large rural-industrial communities near metropolitan centers, designed to improve the housing conditions of workers with low or moderate incomes. The Reconstruction Finance Corpora-

49 The Home Owners Loan Corporation was established prior to 1933.

tion seeks to bolster the market for sound mortgages on urban income-producing property, by refinancing existing mortgages and making loans on new construction where there is economic need for it. Four other agencies are important subsidiaries of the Federal Home Loan Bank Board.[50]

The activities of several of these agencies overlap. Attempts to bring them into an integrated pattern of federal housing policy have been going on for several years. The report of the National Resources Board in December, 1934, mentioned the importance of coordination of effort looking to a better understanding of the methods and scope of each endeavor. Subsequently Mr. Frederic A. Delano, vice-chairman of the National Resources Board, has been the leading spirit in the movement toward coordination. In 1935 he engineered first an informal conference on housing, attended by representatives of both private and governmental agencies, and thereafter a committee of federal housing officials to prepare a report on the possibility of coordination. The report of this committee, submitted to Mr. Delano on May 24, 1935, contained four conclusions.

1. There is a general lack of information among executive officers of federal agencies interested in housing as to what the other agencies in the same field are planning or doing.
2. There is a vast amount of unused general and technical information and experience which has been accumulated at public expense whose translation into more fruitful accomplishment is dependent upon new avenues of release and cooperative action.
3. There is an eager desire among executives of housing agencies to understand the work of kindred agencies and to exchange useful information.

50 The U. S. Housing Authority, created in October, 1937, as a division of the Department of Interior (Public No. 412, 75th Congress, approved September 1, 1937), represents a definite attempt to provide housing for low-income groups. By Executive Order 7732 (October 27, 1937), President Roosevelt transferred to the Authority all the housing and slum-clearance projects of the Federal Emergency Administration of Public Works.

4. There is a noteworthy absence of selfish considerations, ulterior designs and of organizational or professional jealousies. On the contrary, there exists an open handed readiness to give and take freely as a means of accomplishing greater results in the interests of public service.

The conference also produced the recommendation that a Central Housing Committee be created, " . . . to carry out a program of coordination and cooperation along the following general lines:

A. Study the distinctions of purpose and divisions of responsibility among the Government's housing agencies so as to suggest a means of preventing over-centralization, overlapping, duplication, misunderstandings and confusion.
B. Establishment of representative coordinating committees to continue the free exchange of information concerning departmental activities, experiences and results, with provision for regular conferences of executives engaged in kindred work as a means of encouraging coordination and active cooperation.
C. Maintenance of a central clearing house for collecting and disseminating information about what is being planned and done by public and private housing agencies in the United States and abroad.

Mr. Delano took the report to the White House, on May 27, 1935, and suggested that some sort of permanent or recognized status be given to the committee which had prepared it. After a series of conferences, the President gave tentative approval to the plan. On August 29, 1935, he wrote out a four-line memorandum establishing the Central Housing Committee. The memorandum, which never got beyond the longhand stage, read as follows:

1. Continue Committee on coordination of Housing activities.
2. F. A. Delano to continue as chairman.
3. Add P. Grimm to committee and make him assistant to F. A. Delano.

4. Allot $10,000 for executive secretary and staff of stenographers for one year.

The personnel of the committee consisted of one representative from each of the agencies concerned, plus one official alternate.[51] The President's memorandum appointed Mr. Delano as chairman. All other details of organization were worked out by a Subcommittee on Organization, headed by Mr. Coleman Woodbury, Director of the National Association of Housing Officials.

The central committee appointed eight permanent subcommittees.[52] An executive secretariat was organized, including a full-time executive secretary for the central committee and for each of the subcommittees. Additional clerical assistance

51 The original membership of the central committee was as follows: Secretary of Commerce Daniel C. Roper, and Dr. Lyman J. Briggs; W. I. Myers, head of Farm Credit Administration, with Mr. Herbert Emmerich; Col. Horatio B. Hackett, Public Works Administration, with Mr. A. R. Clas; Mr. John H. Fahey, head of the Federal Home Loan Bank Board, with Mr. Ormond E. Loomis; Mr. Stewart McDonald, head of Federal Housing Administration, with Mr. Miles Colean; Mr. Lyle T. Alverson, of the National Emergency Council, with Lt.-Com. C. H. Cotter; Admiral C. J. Peoples, head of the Procurement Division of the Treasury, with Mr. N. Max Dunning; Mr. Rexford G. Tugwell, head of the Resettlement Administration, with Mr. John Lansill; Mr. John W. Slacks, head of the RFC Mortgage Corporation, with Mr. George B. Williams; and Mr. Frederic A. Delano, chairman of the committee.

52 The central committee held its organization meeting on September 27, 1935, and thereafter met 27 times, at intervals of three or four weeks, up to April, 1937. The Subcommitee on Research and Statistics held 36 meetings up to February 2, 1937. The Subcommittee on Planning and Initiation held 12 meetings to June 16, 1936, and was then abolished. The Subcommitee on Operation and Management held 10 meetings between November 7, 1935 and October 16, 1936. The Subcommittee on Procedure and Administration held 19 meetings up to March 19, 1937. The Subcommittee on Review and Information held nine meetings between December 5, 1935 and July 2, 1936 when it disbanded. The Subcommittee on Appraisal and Purchase held 12 meetings between November 8, 1935 and August 12, 1936, and was then reconstituted as the Subcommittee on Appraisal and Mortgage Analysis. The Subcommittee on Design and Construction held 20 meetings between October 28, 1935 and February 3, 1937. The Subcommittee on Land Use and Site Planning held six meetings between January 21, 1937 and April 1, 1937.

was provided as need arose. The Committee has never been supplied with funds, although its authorization mentioned an allotment of $10,000 for one year for clerical help. Its secretariat has been furnished on a contributory basis by the participating agencies. The Committee reported to the President through Mr. Delano, one report being submitted on January 30, 1936, and a second on March 6, 1936.

All the committee meetings were luncheon meetings, at which housing problems were freely discussed in an informal atmosphere. Meetings usually lasted about two hours in all. Typically, the committee listened to the report of its executive secretary, parcelled out assignments of research problems to its subcommittees, received the reports of its subcommittees and approved their recommendations, and occasionally discussed in a desultory fashion the problems of federal responsibility in housing. At one meeting, for example, the committee agreed that preference in federal assistance to housing should be given to localities conforming to " satisfactory standards " of building and planning. It also agreed that no agency should supply at public expense any housing which private enterprise might be " able and willing to provide adequately." Finally it arranged to refer all new bills relating to housing and housing finance to its Subcommittee on Law and Legislation for an expression of opinion. Even after the committee's report revealed its recognition of the major differences in policy among the agencies, the quality of the discussion did not change. If anything it became more perfunctory and more time was given to listening amiably over the coffee while the reports of subcommittees were read.

Meetings of the subcommittees also seem to have been perfunctory. The Subcommittee on Research and Statistics was given the task of analyzing the work being done or contemplated by each of the research and statistical division of the housing agencies, to eliminate overlapping and duplication, to suggest improved techniques for collecting data, and to indicate major gaps in present research activity. The subcommittee met at weekly intervals and appointed a number of sub-committees to make special studies. It was the most prolific of the subcommittees in turning out mimeographed memoranda, but beyond the perfunctory exchange of information little seems to have been accomplished.

The Subcommittee on Planning and Initiation had a threefold assignment: to prepare a descriptive list of projects now under way or pending in the various housing agencies; to analyze and evaluate existing information and current studies of economic forces affecting housing; and to compare the information collected by each of the agencies, making suggestions for increasing the effectiveness of local advice and experience in planning and initiation of housing projects. This subcommittee might have gone far toward achieving cooperation in practice, but it was handicapped by a fluctuating membership. Its activity was confined to the elimination of the most glaring cases of overlapping and conflict, and to a confidential exchange of procedures and criteria already developed by the several agencies. The subcommittee has now been abolished.

The first task of the Subcommittee on Law and Legislation was an informal codification of existing and pending legislation regarding housing. It tried to go beyond routine cataloguing, and set up subcommittees for study of such topics as City Planning and Zoning, Administration of Taxes, and the moratorium question. Committee members sought not only a digest of the law but also a statement of the economic and social effects of existing conditions and recommendations for improvement. This work is still going on, and certain incidental benefits have resulted. On one occasion an interchange of briefs was effected between the Federal Home Loan Bank Board and the Farm Credit Administration, and a conflict of policies was thus forestalled. The subcommittee has sponsored a weekly digest of housing law and legislative proposals which has been welcomed by all the agencies, and which has been made available to the public.

The Subcommittee on Procedure and Administration set out to provide for the exchange of information on rules, regulations and operating procedures, and to study the housing needs and accomplishments of all types of agencies both in the United States and Europe. This was presumably the policy-framing subcommittee. The principal topic of its discussion was the consideration of remedies for the criticism that government action was hampering private initiative and that the federal government had no clearly defined housing program. The subcommittee took one significant step, preparing a confidential summary of the views on federal housing held by the several agencies. The summary was submitted to the central committee and made the basis of the first report to the President.[53] However, no agreement was ever reached on any of the major points at issue. It will be interesting to review these issues, since they represent the core of the still-unsolved problem of coordination in housing policy.

First, should the government deal with housing for low-income groups who cannot afford to pay for adequate housing? Should a long-term program be adopted or should such aid be confined to the emergency? What should be done about slum elimination? Should the government provide subsidies or grants to pay continuing deficits on municipal low-cost housing with differential rentals, selecting the occupants of such structures, and providing better housing for low-income groups than higher-income groups can afford? Should the federal government be merely a demonstration agent in the construction of low-cost housing projects? Should it sponsor limited dividend corporations?

Second, should the government deal with general housing for self-supporting families, and if so how? What encouragement should be given to state and municipal planning? What attention should be given to construction, and what steps should be

53 January 30, 1936. This was a mimeographed report, and was never made public.

taken in tax reforms and in controlling land speculation? How may the evil results of a boom in building be obviated? What controls should the government set up to establish minimum standards for moderate priced housing? To what extent should the government seek uniformity in municipal and state housing legislation? How far should the government go in direct lending or credit guarantees to stimulate private initiative and increase personal security in home financing?

Third, should the Central Housing Committee undertake to clarify the entire housing problem and present suggestions for a federal housing policy to the President? What, in specific terms, should be the committee's basic purpose and program? Should all proposed legislation on housing and home financing be referred to the committee for recommendation before receiving administrative sanction?

In the course of its investigations, it became very clear to the Subcommittee on Procedure and Administration that the participating agencies did not want the Central Housing Committee to " state or intimate what the policies of the government should be " in regard to housing. For example, several agencies did not like to have the central committee send out any printed material. It was felt that the material would look authoritative although the committee had no actual authority to speak for the administration as a whole. The policy of the Resettlement Administration on low-cost housing was not looked upon with approval by some of the other agencies in the housing committee, and when the committee prepared a pamphlet, " Summary of Important Facts on Housing ", for the Council of State Governments, the views of the Resettlement Administration were not represented. A violent controversy ensued. Mr. Tugwell, then head of the Resettlement Administration, stopped coming to meetings because he felt that the central committee had exceeded its proper scope. Nevertheless, when the Subcommittee on Procedure and Administration submitted its report, the existence of controversy was completely ignored.

The Subcommittee on Appraisal and Purchase had the task of arranging for immediate exchange of records and experience in the appraisal and purchase of land, both for the purpose of developing standards and for cooperating with public and private agencies in improving appraisal practices. This was a technical field, narrow in scope. The subcommittee collected a vast amount of material, including a confidential list of all appraisers working for the federal government, but its discussions simply marked time. It was finally absorbed into a new Subcommittee on Appraisal and Mortgage Analysis.

The Subcommittee on Design and Construction arranged for digesting and distributing among the constituent agencies reports of the most significant experience of each with site planning and building construction, to determine minimum and desirable standards in housing design, and to report upon related questions. The subcommittee set up four research groups and turned out several mimeographed bulletins.

The Subcommittee on Operation and Management undertook the ambitious program of exploring the successful financial and social operation of housing projects. The personnel of this group were primarily interested in the technical aspects of housing management. Thus the program outlined by the subcommittee stressed such problems as the simplification of accounting procedures, the investment and depreciation of reserves, simplification of financial reports, and maintenance problems.

The Subcommittee on Review and Information was the public relations group of the Central Housing Committee. It was successful in evading the issue of centralized publicity, as of course was necessary so long as there was no single housing policy within the administration. At one of its meetings the subcommittee reported to the central committee as follows. " . . . It has become apparent that its (the subcommittee's) proper activity is to interpret the work and objectives of the Central Housing Committee and its other subcommittees, and not to initiate public relations undertakings on its own account. The work of this Subcommittee, in our opinion, should be advisory rather than administrative." Though the subcommittee was undoubtedly correct in insisting that it could not publicize a program of the central committee until program and policy were clearly defined, its attitude sometimes bordered on the naïve. For example, when a newspaper article attacking the Resettlement Administration was copied and circularized by the National Retail Lumber Dealers' Association, the committee declared that no attack by "hostile" newspapers or "interested" industrial groups should be considered "worth noticing." The Subcommittee on Review and Information reflected the disagreement among the constituent agencies more sharply, perhaps, than most of the other subcommittees. In the end, it recommended that this sort of work might better be done by a single man than by a group, and preferably by an able public relations man hired expressly for the purpose. The subcommittee was abolished, and no further attempt to integrate public relations was made by the housing agencies.

An interesting experiment was tried by the President in 1935, when he sent Mr. Peter Grimm, a real estate operator of New York City, to interview the field officials of the major housing agencies in six states.[54] According to President Roosevelt's letter, "The purpose of the conference will be to correlate all such activities in a sustained effort to promote the early release of private and public funds for investment in mortgages and construction of needed homes and community facilities." Mr. Grimm, who was a member of the Central Housing Committee in the capacity of assistant to Mr. Delano, recommended in this report the creation of a Federal Housing Coordination Board with definite authority such as the Central Housing Committee did not have. The report also made concrete suggestions as to the future of all the housing agencies. None of these recommendations was given effect.

54 Mr. Grimm is president of William A. White and Sons, a real estate corporation in New York City.

Two reports were made by the central committee to President Roosevelt. Neither report went much further than to point out the areas of disagreement among the heads of the several housing agencies—something with which President Roosevelt must already have been all too familiar. The atmosphere of futility which surrounded these two reports is indicated by a significant statement contained in the first one. "No agreement has yet been reached among members of the Committee on two points, (1) the extent to which the Federal Government shall continue to assume the burden of finance or construction, and (2) the proper line of demarcation between the fields of public and private activity." [55] The second report suggested that gains in understanding had been made, but its specific statements were not encouraging. The report consisted entirely of vague generalizations which could not possibly be made the basis for a consistent housing policy.

Evaluation of the Central Housing Committee turns upon the query, Was there, at this time, a deliberate will in the Administration not to make a clear choice among housing methods? Two things seem clear. First, the housing committee was set up to survey the problems of coordination rather than to construct a federal housing policy. Second, hope was nevertheless held out that the committee might lay the foundations of a federal housing policy, by clarifying the points at issue among the various agencies and also by leading housing administrators to understand and appreciate each others' endeavors. The Central Housing Committee has now been in existence for three years, and it is safe to say that the committee has not produced the results that might have been anticipated from the amount of time and energy expended by members. The committee and its subsidiary groups have accumulated a great deal of informative material. In the interpretation and creative use of this material, the committee has, however, been conspicuously weak.[56]

55 Report of January 30, 1936.

56 For example, when the Wagner Housing bill was under consideration

It is difficult to assign specific reasons for the inadequacies of the Housing Committee. Impressive coordinating machinery was built up, but the wheels never turned smoothly. Somehow, things never seemed to click into place. There was a hollow ring to all the committee's proceedings which suggests a lack of effectiveness in the executive secretariats of the parent committee and subcommittees. Diligence was not lacking, but it was unimaginative and plodded along in routine paths. Apparently the secretariat could not supply the creative element in staff work, the presentation of issues and alternatives in such a way that differences are reconciled and new policies formulated.

in 1935, President Roosevelt asked the Central Housing Committee for information and advice regarding the coordination of federal housing activities. The Committee was unable to furnish him with what he wanted, much to his disappointment.

CHAPTER IV

INSTITUTIONAL COORDINATING COMMITTEES

To distinguish between the functional and the institutional aspects of public administration is to contrast the objectives or ends of governmental action with the methods or means by which it is made possible.[1] No matter what activity a governmental agency may undertake, there are a number of operations in which it must inevitably engage. Employees must be hired and ways found to obtain maximum efficiency from them. This is personnel management. Supplies of all sorts must be purchased, such as typewriters, filing cabinets, room furnishings, and all the materials used in conducting the particular governmental service. This is procurement or matériel management. The costs of operating the agency must be planned and the money for operations spent in accordance with the budget. This is fiscal management. These three examples illustrate the type of activity sometimes called the institutional, or, more popularly, the housekeeping aspects of administration. The housekeeping aspects of administration are a narrow, though indispensable, set of auxiliary technical activities which make possible the exercise of the government's functions or the furnishing of governmental services.

There is an obvious sameness about all housekeeping activities. Each functional activity, however, is unique. Consequently, it is much easier to coordinate the means than the ends of public administration. To be sure, departments will protest

1 "Analysis of the duties or working activities of an administrative service shows that they fall into two clearly distinguishable classes: those which the service has to perform in order that it may exist and operate as an organization or institution, and those that it must perform in order to accomplish the ends for which it has been established and is being maintained. These two classes of activities may be designated as institutional and functional." W. F. Willoughby, *Principles of Public Administration* (Brookings Institution, Washington, D. C., 1927), pp. 45-46.

against the centralization of procurement, personnel management and fiscal management. Each will complain that its peculiar problems require the judgment of an individual actually participating in its work in order to hire effective employees or select just the right type of filing cabinet. It is therefore common practice to accompany the process of horizontal integration by some method of consulting the agencies affected. Procurement, for example, has been centralized in the Treasury Department for several years. Uniform regulations govern this activity in all federal agencies. A supplementary structure of advisory committees provides for interdepartmental consultation in framing the regulations issued by the Treasury's Procurement Division.[2] Another example of interdepartmental cooperation in administrative housekeeping is the Council of Personnel Administration, which brings together the departmental personnel officers to investigate and recommend improved personnel policies and procedures. The Council of Personnel Administration "has organized and prosecuted a number of studies, but has achieved its greatest success in the development of an improved efficiency rating system, which was placed in effect in the departmental service at Washington by order of the Civil Service Commission in 1935. . . . The limited experience with the present Council does appear to indicate that important values can result from well-organized consultation between the central personnel agency and the personnel officers of operating establishments." [3]

Certain activities, though essentially administrative housekeeping, closely resemble the functional aspects of public administration. Among these is the preparation of governmental

2 For a description of the interdepartmental organization of procurement in the national administration, see Charles A. Beard, *The American Leviathan* (The Macmillan Company, New York, 1931), pp. 370-375.

3 Floyd W. Reeves and Paul T. David, "Personnel Administration in the Federal Service," in *Report and Special Studies*, President's Committee on Administrative Management (Washington, D. C., 1937), pp. 84 ff. The Council of Personnel Administration was reconstituted and its status clarified by an Executive Order of June 24, 1938.

statistics. The actual collection of statistics is a matter of mechanical routine. Certain statistics are compiled and used solely for administrative purposes.[4] Other statistics are collected and issued to meet public demands for information regarding the economic and social progress of the country.[5] These latter statistics are more than a mere by-product of departmental operations; ideally considered, they should become the foundation of adequate machinery for thinking.

The advantages of centralizing the compilation of statistics are outweighed in the minds of administrators by the firm entrenchment of decentralization.[6] Perhaps the most generally accepted advantages of consolidation are those resulting from the elimination of overlapping and duplication of effort. The quality of the statistics gathered is improved when uniform schedules are used by all agencies. Data gathered by one agency are made available to other agencies in usable form. The demands which statistical agencies make upon business, industry, and other private sources of information are reduced to a minimum, with a consequent tendency for the public to look more favorably upon this phase of governmental activity.

A further advantage of centralized supervision of statistics is that the government and the general public are provided with a single authoritative source of official information. The necessity for such a source of information becomes most apparent in times of national crisis. In time of war, and during economic depression, confusion may result from the lack of correct and authoritative information. Even when no emergency exists,

4 *E. g.*, those compiled by the Social Security Board as part of its normal operations.

5 *E. g.*, those compiled by the staff and consultants of the National Resources Committee in connection with its report, *Technological Trends and National Policy* (Washington, D. C., 1937).

6 For a classic statement of the case for centralization, see *Report on the Collection and Presentation of Official Statistics*, prepared by a Committee appointed by the Cabinet under the chairmanship of Sir Alfred W. Watson (London, 1921).

administration can be demoralized and effective leadership becomes difficult when two departments issue conflicting reports.

The Central Statistical Board is the latest in a series of attempts to coordinate official statistical inquiry. It represents a policy somewhere between the extremes of centralization and decentralization. The Board does not depend solely on voluntary cooperation, yet neither does it have full administrative authority over its constituent agencies.

Central Statistical Board [7]

The earliest recognition of the need for centralizing the compilation of official statistics developed as part of the drive for a permanent census office. The demand for such an office became articulate during the census of 1870. A series of studies of the

7 The Central Statistical Board was selected for analysis in a case study primarily because the activity of compiling statistics is a borderline one. The experience of the Board offers constructive suggestions for coordination both in the managerial and in the functional aspects of administration. Moreover, this is an example of the interdepartmental committee when it is well past the experimental stage, yet one in which the process of coordination is portrayed in those early, formative phases which are the most interesting and significant.

Other interdepartmental committees which have been concerned with the managerial or housekeeping aspects of administration are as follows:

Federal Contract Board.
Federal Standard Stock Catalog Board.
Federal Specifications Board.
Interdepartmental subcommittees of Federal Specifications Board.
Committee on Paper Specifications.
Interdepartmental Committee on Envelopes.
Communications Coordination Committee.
Aviation Procurement Committee.
Army-Navy Aircraft Standards Committee.
Army-Navy Munitions Board.
Commodity Committees of Army-Navy Munitions Board.
Standardization and Specification Division of Army-Navy Munitions Board.
Price Control Division of Army-Navy Munitions Board.
Labor Division of Army-Navy Munitions Board.
Power Division of Army-Navy Munitions Board.
Legal and Contracts Division of Army-Navy Munitions Board.
Transportation Division of Army-Navy Munitions Board.

problem were made, in which certain fundamental ideas were enunciated.[8]

Under our political system, with its wide distribution of jurisdiction among states, counties, cities, and towns, and with the vast private initiative which characterizes American life, the data, upon whose collection and incorporation into one homogeneous whole, all sound statistical generalization and scientific deduction depends are so fragmentary and scattered that the need of centralization of statistical inquiry is sorely felt. Such centralization can only be effected by the National Government, and the Government itself is powerless to accomplish this result without the intervention of a central bureau, thoroughly scientific in its character and methods.

It seems clear that Congress, recognizing the need for a central statistical bureau, intended to concentrate in the Census Office the compilation of all statistics not intimately connected with departmental administrative operations. The debates regarding the legislation for the permanent census office, and also those preceding the establishment of the Department of Commerce and Labor, of which the Census Office was made a part, all point to this conclusion.

The first step toward interdepartmental coordination of statistics came in 1908, when an interdepartmental statistical committee consisting of representatives of the several departments and the Interstate Commerce Commission was established by Executive Order. This committee interpreted its

Facilities Division of Army-Navy Munitions Board.
Joint Economy Board, Army and Navy.
The Codification Board (for Federal Register).
Council of Personnel Administration.
Federal Fire Council.
Fire Record Committee.
Fire Hazard Committee.
Legal Committee.
National Archives Council.
Interdepartment Radio Advisory Committee.

8 *The Census Office and Coordination of Statistics*, Government Printing office (Washington, D. C., 1909), p. 5.

function as merely the preparation of a report and recommendations on the problem. A survey was made of the work of all statistical agencies of the federal government. Several instances of duplication were found. As a result of the committee's report, voluntary cooperation among the statistical agencies was increased but no official action was taken in the direction of general interdepartmental consolidation.[9]

During the World War, however, the need for a coordinating agency became urgent, and a Central Bureau of Planning and Statistics was organized in the War Industries Board.[10] This bureau acted as an advisory body to other statistical agencies, and as a clearing house for statistical information. It also assembled and organized statistical data and planned and directed most of the government's statistical work. The functions of the Central Bureau of Planning and Statistics were transferred to the Bureau of Efficiency in 1918, and a survey was then made of federal statistical services. The Bureau of Efficiency recommended the consolidation of many of the statistical units into a single organization. The recommendation was not put into effect, however, and the experiment in coordination came to an end.

The crisis years after 1929 once again made obvious the need for integration, and in 1931 a Federal Statistical Board was established under the Bureau of the Budget. This organization had no staff, and was able to make only a limited, though valuable, contribution to the problem. It was replaced in July, 1933, by the Central Statistical Board, five members of the old board becoming members of the new. The new group worked continuously for statutory authorization, which was

9 See *Reply of the Director of the Census to the Inquiries of the Interdepartmental Statistical Committee*, January 8, 1909 (Washington, Government Printing Office, 1909).

10 For a description of the Central Bureau of Planning and Statistics, see F. L. Paxson, "The American War Government, 1917-1918, *American Historical Review*, Vol. XXVI (October, 1920), pp. 54-76. See also Lloyd M. Short, *Development of National Administrative Organization in the United States* (University of Illinois Press, Urbana, 1923), p. 449.

finally given to them in 1935. The organization which now coordinates the statistical services of the federal government was authorized by an Act of Congress approved July 25, 1935, and was set up under Executive Order No. 7287, February 10, 1936.

In providing for coordination of the statistical services, Congress set up two agencies, a Central Statistical Committee and a Central Statistical Board. The Central Statistical Committee is nominally the over-all coordinating agency for all federal statistical inquiry. When Donald Richberg was Executive Director of the National Emergency Council, he brought about the creation of this committee as an attempt to narrow the channel of access to the President by interposing a group of Cabinet officials between the President and the Central Statistical Board. The statute specifies that the Secretaries of Labor, Commerce, Treasury and Agriculture shall be members of the Central Statistical Committee. The Committee has had only one or two formal meetings, since it has been found difficult to get the members together. Ordinarily the chairman of the Committee, Secretary of Labor Perkins, asks the members to stay on after Cabinet meetings when there is some specific matter to be acted upon.

The Central Statistical Board is the real center of operations in the coordination of statistical work. By section 5 of the statute, it is provided that " The Board shall:

(a) At the request of the President or the Committee, or may of its own motion, investigate and make recommendations with respect to any existing or proposed statistical work carried on by an agency of, or subject to the supervision of, the Federal Government:

(b) Have the power, with the consent of the agency concerned, to investigate and make recommendations with respect to any existing or proposed statistical work carried on by any agency in the United States other than the agencies specified in subsection (a) of this section:

(c) Plan and promote the economical operation of agencies concerned in statistical work and the elimination of unnecessary work on the part of such agencies and on the part of persons called on by such agencies to furnish information;

(d) Perform such other duties consistent with section 1 of this Act as the President or the Committee may authorize, and make such reports to the Committee as the Committee may require.

The chairman of the Board is appointed by the President with the advice and consent of the Senate.[11] In conformity with Executive Order, six of the 13 additional members of the Board are designated, respectively, by the Secretaries of the Treasury, Interior, Agriculture, Labor, Commerce, and the Chairman of the Board of Governors of the Federal Reserve System. The remaining seven members are elected by the chairman and the six designated members. No term is specified for the chairman, other than the automatic limitation of the five-year duration given the Board by statute. Designated members hold office at the pleasure of the officer appointing them, with the provision that their terms shall not exceed two years without redesignation. Elected members hold office for two years, subject to removal by the President. Membership is conditioned upon retaining employment in the federal agency from which elected, and vacancies are filled for the unexpired term.

11 The membership of the Central Statistical Board, as of November 1, 1938, is as follows: Stuart A. Rice, chairman; Isador Lubin, Department of Labor, first vice-chairman (A. Ford Hinrichs, Alternate); Richard C. Patterson, Department of Commerce (Malcolm Kerlin, Alternate); Mordecai Ezekiel, Department of Agriculture (Louis H. Bean, Alternate); A. Goldenweiser, Board of Governors of the Federal Reserve System (Woodlief Thomas, Alternate); George C. Haas, Department of the Treasury (Russell R. Reagh, Alternate); Oscar E. Kiessling, Department of the Interior); Arthur J. Altmeyer, Social Security Board (Ewan Clague, Alternate); E. Dana Durand, U. S. Tariff Commission (L. A. Morrison, Alternate); Ernest M. Fisher, Federal Housing Administration (Warren Jay Vinton, Alternate); Corrington Gill, Works Progress Administration (Emerson Ross, Alternate); Clyde L. Seavey, Federal Power Commission (Charles W. Smith, Alternate); Frederick F. Stephan, American Statistical Association; Oscar C. Stine, Department of Agriculture (Frederick L. Thomsen, Alternate).

The relationship of the Committee to the Board is somewhat ambiguous. In practice it seems likely that the Board will use the Committee, rather than the Committee direct the work of the Board in any way. The first formal activity of the Committee was its official announcement, in 1936, that the Central Statistical Board had been organized. A statement to this effect was published in the Federal Register over the signatures of the four members of the Committee. This was the Committee's only activity in 1936. Subsequently, the Central Statistical Committee has promulgated the rules and regulations which the Board has drafted. For example, Regulation No. 1 governed the submission for review of questionnaires, plans, and the like by the various statistical agencies to the Board. These regulations are, of course, drawn up by the Board and the signature of the Committee is a mere formality. In fact, the formal announcement of regulations could be made by the Board—section 5c of the statute gives it ample authority—but the Board feels that its position is strengthened by using the Committee.

It was originally intended that in day-to-day business the Central Statistical Committee should function as the Board's primary contact with the President, but the probability is strong that the Cabinet group will be only one channel of communication with the White House and that the most formal. Since the chairman of the Board is appointed by the President he feels that he at least has the right to report directly to the President if he chooses. When Winfield Riefler was both economic advisor to the National Emergency Council and chairman of the Board, its reports were made through the National Emergency Council. However, the Central Statistical Board's functions were at that time interpreted as including assistance to its chairman in furnishing current economic information to the Council, a procedure which has now been subordinated to the function of coordinating the statistical services. With this restriction upon its duties the necessity for contact with the President diminished, but the entreé to the White House has never been lost and continues to be an important factor in the Board's work. For example after Stuart Rice took office as chairman in the spring of 1936, the Central Statistical Board came to the conclusion that WPA statistical projects involving doorbell ringing were becoming so frequent as to lower the prestige of government statistical work. The steering committee set up to coordinate the activities of WPA and the Central Statistical Board adopted a no-canvassing rule. This rule was not strictly observed and finally Dr. Rice wrote a letter to the President asking that the rule be given Presidential sanction. The letter was read at a National Emergency Council meeting and President Roosevelt, without any discussion of the matter, simply stated that he concurred with the Board's views. The rule was thereafter observed by the agencies concerned.

The Central Statistical Board handles both policy and operating matters; there is no division on these lines between the Board and its governing committee. The Board meets formally once a month, except during the summer, and occasionally it holds special meetings on subjects of general interest to which it invites statistical experts and other guests. Minutes of meetings and complete files are kept by the Board's staff. Although most of the members of the Board hold positions of high rank and heavy responsibility in their respective departments, attendance at meetings has been very regular. A frequent practice is for both principals and alternates to attend. The Board employs a permanent secretariat, a small research staff, and clerical help in varying degrees.

Since the fiscal year 1936, when the Board received statutory authorization, an annual appropriation of funds has been made for its work. Before 1936, most of the expense items were carried by other agencies. A partial allotment of funds was made in 1934 and 1935, but this did not cover such important items as the cost of the chairmanship and the chairman's staff, the cost of the Board's fiscal work, the cost of staff work by the Committee on Government Statistics, and the cost of the Division of Current Business Statistics.[12]

The role of the executive secretary is flexible and of considerable responsibility. He is in constant communication with the chairman, who is by law "the chief executive of the Board." As a working arrangement their positions are interchangeable, since the secretary is thoroughly familiar with the details of the chairman's work. Morris A. Copeland is the Board's executive secretary, chief of staff and director of its technical work. The by-laws of the Board provide that the executive secretary shall be secretary of the Board's standing committees; he also acts as secretary of most of the Board's subject-matter committees, and in some cases he is chairman. Through this procedure the executive secretary has been a very effective instrument of coordination.

The Board has two standing committees, one on Policy and one on Organization and Budget.[13] It is the task of the Committee on General Policy to give preliminary consideration to problems of Board policy. From time to time the Committee on General Policy has temporarily exercised certain general functions on behalf of the Board; for example, the Board delegated to this committee the authority to supervise inquiries into the costs of statistical services. The Committee on Organization and Budget plans the Board's organization and procedure so far as administrative details are concerned. It supervises the finances of the Board, and supervises all staff appointments except that of Executive Secretary.

The core of the Board's task is the critical review of statistical schedules. In this phase of the Board's work its principal

12 For a tabulation of the Board's principal items of expense, see its *Annual Report* (U. S. Government Printing Office, Washington, D. C.), for 1936 and the years following.

13 Originally there were five standing committees. In addition to the two described above, there was a Committee on Techniques of Collection and Tabulation, a Committee on Clearance of Statistical Releases, and Committees on Techniques of Statistical Analysis.

instrument of coordination is the subject matter committee. These committees are numerous, their duties varied, and the scope of their authority generally flexible.[14]

One type of subject matter committee is used to eliminate duplication of effort among statistical agencies. A typical instance is the field of power statistics, where the Power Commission, the Geological Survey, and the Bureau of the Census were all overlapping. When the Board becomes aware of such a situation it appoints a member of its permanent staff to study the problem and become thoroughly aware of all its aspects. In the course of the study, a program is prepared which draws together the work of the different agencies. Then, accompanied either by the executive secretary or the chairman of the Board, the staff member discusses the situation with the heads of the agencies involved and gets their approval for the establishment of a committee. The Central Statistical Board actually sets up the committee, calling on each agency to name a member, but the committee is formally organized only after informal consultation and approval by the interested agencies. The execu-

14 Among the subject matter committees which functioned in 1934-35 were the following: a Committee on a Survey of Unemployment, established to investigate methods that should be employed in unemployment surveys and to make definite recommendations on the nature and time of an unemployment census; a Committee on Census Survey, established at the request of the Director of the Bureau of the Census, to conduct a comprehensive survey of the Divisions of Manufactures, Agriculture, Population, and Vital Statistics, and the personnel and organization of the Bureau of the Census; a Committee on Industries under Codes, established to plan and promote improvements in current statistics on industries under codes; a Committee on Foreign Trade Statistics, established to consider various problems arising in regard to the foreign trade statistics of the United States; a Committee on retail prices and cost-of-living studies, established to promote the coordination and improvement of retail price statistics and family expenditure and budget studies; a similar Committee on construction and real property statistics; and an interim committee on national-income estimates, established to plan for a centralized estimate of national income on a monthly basis and for a further division of labor in the annual estimates of national income. These descriptions are taken from the First Annual Report of the Central Statistical Board, for the year ended December 31, 1934 (Government Printing Office, Washington, 1934), Appendix F.

tive secretary of the Board then takes the position either of chairman or secretary of the new committee, depending on the situation. If it is a very delicate one he will take the chairmanship, but if the likelihood of achieving agreement is strong he will simply take the secretaryship. In most cases, since the situation will previously have been canvassed and the job thoroughly outlined, the committee's program will at once be put into effect, unless some special reasons make such action inexpedient. The proposed policy is referred back to the agencies for approval, the work is begun immediately, and the committee disbands when the task is completed.

A second type of subject matter committee is exploratory. In such cases the committee does not adopt a program which has already been worked out, but rather discusses a proposed policy, seeking to reconcile viewpoints. Establishment of the committee is followed, rather than preceded, by staff work. The personnel of such committees is most frequently drawn direct from the membership of the Central Statistical Board, with representatives of other agencies occasionally being appointed where such agencies are not represented on the Board.

A third type of committee (which is now growing rare) uses no staff work at all, but acts only in and through committee sessions. Here again the membership includes Board members or their alternates. A typical example is the Committee on Techniques of Collection, which reviewed schedules in committee meetings and did the actual work of altering the schedules, *inter alia,* of the Bureau of Labor Statistics.

A fourth type is the straight conference, which in some cases leads to the establishment of an inter-agency committee by the conferring officials rather than by the Board. For example, in 1935 a conference on a census of unemployment was called by the Central Statistical Board, and the conference group itself established an inter-agency committee to integrate the agencies participating in the census. The conference, and later the committee, laid the foundations for the unemployment census which was finally taken in 1937. The committee functioned for more than a year, under the chairmanship of Isador Lubin. It included in its membership representatives from the Bureau of the Census, the Bureau of Agricultural Economics, the Bureau of Labor Statistics, and other interested agencies. The relationship between this committee and the Central Statistical Board was ambiguous at first, but it was clear that the Board could take it over if necessary since both Mr. Lubin and Mr. Rice were members of the committee and could exert a controlling influence if a show-down should occur. In the end, the Board did take over this committee, and its status became that of one of the Board's ordinary subject-matter committees.

In the early days of its existence, the Central Statistical Board acted as a clearing house of economic information within the administration. Winfield Riefler at this time occupied the dual role of chairman of the Central Statistical Board and Economic Adviser to the National Emergency Council. To provide an accurate, comprehensive digest of economic data for spokesmen for the administration, Mr. Riefler presented a general summary of the economic situation at each Council meeting. Eventually it was found desirable to abolish the Office of Economic Adviser, and its staff was absorbed into the secretariat of the Central Statistical Board. When Stuart Rice succeeded Mr. Riefler as chairman of the Central Statistical Board, he took the position with the express understanding that the furnishing of economic information would be subordinated to the review of statistical schedules. However, there is still some demand from Cabinet officials and members of Congress for current economic information. Consequently, this work is still carried on, though it is no longer one of the Board's major activities. One man, Isador Lubin, holds the two positions of first vice-chairman of the Board and executive secretary of the Central Statistical Committee, and directs this work. The Chief Economist of the Board, Miss Aryness Joy, who worked with Mr. Riefler when he acted as Economic Adviser to the National

Emergency Council, now assists Mr. Lubin in furnishing current economic information.[15]

The decisions taken at the meeting of June 25, 1936, may be cited as typical of the Board's action at meetings.

1. The Board discussed the draft of a regulation relative to submission of questionnaires and other materials for review. This regulation was to be referred to the Central Statistical Committee, along with other rules and regulations, for final action and promulgation.

2. Action was taken to reconstitute the old Committee on Public Assistance Statistics.

3. The chairman was authorized to set up a Committee on Payroll and Employment Reports.

4. Action was taken to put the annual report on a fiscal year basis, and it was decided that the next annual report should cover the period January 1, 1935, to June 30, 1936.

5. The chairman was given authority to execute the decisions of the Board, and to delegate this authority to the secretariat.

6. Preparation of the 1938 budget was referred to the Committee on Organization and Budget.

7. The staff of the Board was commended for its work in assisting the Civil Service Commission in establishing a register for the position of general economist.

The Central Statistical Board is one of the outstanding examples of successful interdepartmental coordination in the period 1932-36. Judged by the criterion of the extent to which its policies have been adopted by the participating departments, its percentage of failure seems to have been negligible. To be sure, the Board's decisions have often been watered down to such an extent as to lose almost all traces of positive authority. However, to say that compromise has marked all the Board's actions is only to emphasize the fact that, in the process of coordination, compromise is often a sign of progress. It is

15 Since this manuscript was completed, Mr. Lubin has ceased to be a member of the Central Statistical Board.

impossible for an effective coordinating agency to proceed without encountering opposition and criticism, but it seems to me that the Board's prestige has been relatively high, especially in administrative circles.[16]

Much of the Board's success is unquestionably due to the brilliant and untiring efforts of its chairman, Stuart Rice, and its executive secretary, Morris Copeland. But credit must go to all the individuals who have participated in the initial establishment and subsequent operation of the Board, for the Central Statistical Board shows the results of conscientious and intelligent workmanship in all its phases. The Board's procedure represents the perfect adjustment of organization to function. The phase of discussion and conversation is wisely kept within small groups. At the same time, the Board has never tried to maintain an atmosphere of secrecy. The organization is flexible enough to adapt itself to varying situations, yet it is authoritative when decision becomes necessary.

16 The Board has had some difficulty in securing the appropriations needed for its work, particularly in the winter of 1936 when the requested appropriation was cut in half and finally made up only through an allocation of funds from the President's second deficiency appropriation of 1937.

PART II

METHODS

CHAPTER V

PROBLEMS OF ESTABLISHMENT

THE success or failure of an interdepartmental committee depends to a great extent on the circumstances surrounding its creation. The effectiveness of the committee depends upon the clarity with which, at the time it is set up, its objectives are conceived and its structure, personnel and procedures are adapted to these objectives.

There are two major steps to be taken in the process of establishment. The first is the definition of the committee's task. The second is the selection of the officials who are to serve on the committee. Of course these phases are never thought of as separate by the officials who establish the committee, nor can they actually be isolated as two distinct activities. Officials have apparently been quite unaware that in setting up interdepartmental committees they were going through successive stages of a pattern. Nevertheless, the pattern is discernible when one takes a cross-sectional view of interdepartmental committees.

In analyzing the process of defining the committee's task, three elements must be treated in turn. It is first of all necessary to review the types of authorization by which the establishment of an interdepartmental committee is formally announced. Second, one must ask how the decision to set up a committee is actually made. Third, one must examine the several types of situations which have been made the basis for deciding to create an interdepartmental committee.

There are three types of authorization under which interdepartmental committees have been formed. Some groups, like the Central Statistical Board, have been set up by an act of Congress. In a much larger number of cases, the committee has been set up by letter or memorandum from the President to the heads of the agencies involved, or by Executive Order.

The third source of authority has been a letter or memorandum from one department head to another. These three methods have been used indiscriminately, having no particular connection with the objectives of the committee concerned. Indeed, there seems to be no good reason for using a statute instead of presidential authorization. Committees set up by Executive Order have been as important, as successful, and as permanent as those created by Congress.

There is a tendency, nevertheless, for interdepartmental committees to try to move from an informal type of authorization to one that they consider more permanent or stable. The Interdepartment Radio Advisory Committee started its existence under the authority of a letter from the Secretary of Commerce to the heads of the other Executive Departments and of certain independent agencies. The Radio Committee developed a very satisfactory technique for coordination, and the scope of its work was gradually extended by successive Executive Orders. In this case there were definite reasons for using the Executive Order, since the committee was assigned a task which Congress had imposed on the President—the allocation of wavelengths to governmental broadcasting stations. But clear-cut cases of this sort are rare. Many committees which are carrying on a fairly permanent program of coordination or research simply feel that they will operate better under statutory authorization.

Congressional sanction frequently implies a grant of funds to the committee, which tends to free the committee from dependence on its constituent departments and perhaps from domination by one or two of them, thus permitting more satisfactory development of the committee's work. Moreover, congressional sanction is supposed to make the committee a more permanent affair than the group whose existence depends merely on some informal letter or memorandum. The combination of these factors tends to give the committee greater prestige in the administrative structure so that its decisions will more readily be accepted as the policy of those agencies which the committee is trying to coordinate. As an example of the effect of statutory authorization, the experience of the National Advisory Committee on Aeronautics may be cited. This committee started under Executive Order, but has now expanded its work to the point where it uses a million-dollar appropriation annually. The status of the Aeronautics Committee has been recognized by congressional authorization of an appropriation for so many years that it is now practically an independent agency. On the other hand, the experience of the Central Statistical Board indicates that congressional sanction does not fully insure the future of an interdepartmental committee. The Central Statistical Board, originally set up by Executive Order, sought statutory recognition as a safeguard against being liquidated by a change of administration.[1] However, the Board found that the same Congress which had created it later on refused to appropriate any money for its work. The necessary funds were subsequently found in the President's second deficiency appropriation in 1937.

From this review of the possible methods of authorization, it is clear that the formal steps in creating an interdepartmental committee may be taken by Congress, by the President, or by a Department head. But how is the decision to create a committee actually made?

There is always some sort of preliminary scrutiny of the situation. In most cases, however, these first steps toward interdepartmental cooperation are extremely informal. What happens, usually, is the gradual development of an awareness that the relations of certain agencies with each other need to be clarified. Sometimes the bureau chiefs, possibly the departmental management, occasionally the President's secretariat, will recognize a need for interdepartmental action. As a consequence of a telephone conversation or a personal conference between officials of two bureaus, interdepartmental contact is

1 Actually, of course, one type of authorization is no more nor less "safe" than another. Executive Orders do not lose their force with a change of administration.

established. Sometimes an informal interdepartmental liaison develops, which may or may not mature in an interdepartmental committee. Two or three officials, usually at the request of their department heads, will meet at their own convenience, often over the luncheon table, to talk over common problems. They may have their aides put together a statement of facts as a basis for such discussions. If any record is kept, it will be a memorandum summarizing the conversations. Eventually, the officials will report to their chiefs the results of their explorations of the subject. If further interdepartmental action seems necessary, they may recommend that the department heads concerned appoint an interdepartmental committee.

The formation of the Interdepartmental Committee on Civil International Aviation affords an example of the gradual development of an interdepartmental committee from relatively informal beginnings. In 1933 an informal liaison between the Departments of State and Commerce existed to study the problem of drafting reciprocal agreements with foreign countries for the establishment of international air routes. This arrangement was set up by an exchange of letters between the Secretaries of Commerce and State, on October 11, 1933, and lasted until late in 1934. One official was designated from each department; naturally, however, as the conversations progressed other individuals in both departments became conscious of the problem and were drawn into the discussions. Records were kept and facts were amassed. Throughout the spring of 1935, informal negotiations were under way between Imperial Airways, Ltd., of Great Britain, and Pan-American Airways of the United States to establish a passenger air service between Europe and the United States. The governments of both countries were aware of these conferences, and on June 25, 1935, the State Department received a communication from the British Embassy suggesting cooperation between the governments of the United States, France, and England, " In studying the technical aspects of collaboration in trans-Atlantic air transport." Machinery had already been set up in the State Department to study the diplomatic aspects of this new situation.[2] On April 25, 1935, Secretary Hull appointed a State Department committee to consider these matters in cooperation with the chiefs of the geographic divisions.[3] Similar arrangements for study of the problem of international air transport had been made in the Commerce Department. However, the initiative throughout was taken by the Department of State. During this formative period everyone concerned with civil international aviation was aware that the matter was one for concerted interdepartmental action. The State Department was perhaps most directly involved since it would be charged with the negotiation and conclusion of whatever reciprocal agreements were used to establish international air routes. The Commerce Department is required by law to approve matters pertaining to civil aviation within the borders of the United States. The Treasury Department, because of its control over customs and revenue collection, would have to be consulted, and the Post Office would probably wish to arrange for reciprocal carrying of mails. Thus when the point was reached at which the formal negotiations for international air routes could be entered upon, interdepartmental machinery had already been constructed and required only formal sanction. The Interdepartmental Committee on Civil International Aviation was appointed by Presidential memoranudum of July 2, 1935, naming as members four assistant secretaries from the departments involved.[4]

In the foregoing case, informal consultation led to the creation of an interdepartmental committee. Consequently, records were kept of the original liaison. Far more common, however, is the type of informal contact that goes unrecorded.

2 See *Press Release* of May 4, 1935, U. S. State Department.

3 State Department, *Press Release*, July 2, 1935.

4 The members of this committee were as follows:

R. Walton Moore, Assistant Secretary of State, Chairman.
Stephen B. Gibbons, Assistant Secretary of the Treasury.
Harllee Branch, Second Assistant Postmaster General.
John M. Johnson, Assistant Secretary of Commerce.

Assistant secretaries may lunch together, discuss their work, and completely forget the incident. It is a commonplace for bureau chiefs of different departments to call at each others' offices for informal conferences on urgent, though perhaps relatively unimportant matters. The existence and importance of this sort of informal consultation is indicated by even a cursory glance at departmental files, where letters and memoranda continually refer to "the matter which we discussed yesterday morning." The testimony of bureau chiefs confirms the supposition that only a small number of such conversations are thus recorded.

On what basis, then, is the decision made to set up an interdepartmental committee? What are the circumstances which make it desirable to go from the informal to the formal type of interdepartmental consultation?

First, when an Act of Congress or an Executive Order assigns parts of a program to separate agencies, an interdepartmental committee will always be formed. The Trade Agreements Act, for example, specifically mentions that the President "shall seek information and advice . . . from the U. S. Tariff Commission, the Departments of State, Agriculture and Commerce."[5] Another example is the interdepartmental committee which has been concerned with the C. C. C. program. Under the Executive Order which originally provided for the Emergency Conservation Work program, the Chief of Finance of the War Department acted as fiscal manager, applicants for Civilian Conservation Corps enrollment were selected by the Department of Labor, were examined and accepted by the War Department, and were put to work on projects planned by the Departments of Interior, War, and Agriculture, under supervision of the War Department.[6] A third example is

5 The Trade Agreements Act, an amendment to the Smoot-Hawley Tariff Act of 1930, approved June 12, 1934.

6 The Advisory Council for Emergency Conservation Work is the coordinating committee for the C. C. C. program, set up by Executive Order 6101, April 5, 1933.

afforded by the Committee on Airports of Entry. Regulation and supervision of domestic air commerce requires action by three departments, Treasury, Commerce and State, with a fourth, the Department of Agriculture, having important interests involved. The Air Commerce Act,[7] and the Tariff Act of 1930 [8] authorize the Secretary of the Treasury to designate places in the United States as ports of entry for civil aircraft and to apply to civil air navigation appropriate regulations under the customs and public health laws. The Secretary of Commerce is authorized to make regulations governing the entry and clearance of aircraft at the designated airports, and the Secretary of Labor is authorized to designate any of the ports of entry as stations of the U. S. Immigration Service, with appropriate regulations and personnel. No provision is made for the collaboration of the Department of Agriculture's Bureau of Entomology and Plant Quarantine, but consultation with an official of this bureau is customary. In cases where the need for interdepartmental cooperation is so clear-cut as this, the act of creating an interdepartmental committee is almost automatic. A letter from the Secretary of the Treasury to the Secretaries of Labor and Commerce led to the establishment of the Committee on Airports of Entry, with an assistant secretary from each department as members.

Second, when the questions at issue become the subject of acute controversy, an interdepartmental committee has often seemed to be more useful than informal conference. An example is the Industrial Emergency Committee. This group was brought into existence when the Administration's recovery policy needed general reconsideration. The agencies working on the problems of industry, agriculture and relief were at cross purposes in the spring and summer of 1934. A common policy was needed for all the agencies participating in the relief and recovery program.

7 49 USCA 176.

8 U. S. Code, Title 49, sec. 177 (b), (c), and (d); Tariff Act of 1930, sec. 644.

The situation came to a head with the controversy over the "prevailing wage scale" in the matter of wage payments and operating standards affecting the codified industries. The N.R.A. codes merely set minimum wage levels, which in the construction industries tended to benefit only unskilled labor. Labor unions in the construction industries were bringing pressure to bear on N.R.A. administrators, urging that the union rates be written into the codes. There was also a good deal of agitation for F.E.R.A. to pay "the prevailing wage" of a community, which would amount to the wages of skilled labor, to people on work relief. In addition to these complications of policy, George Peek, Administrator of A.A.A. and General Hugh Johnson, Administrator of N.R.A., were continually at swords' points. Neither hesitated to deliver a scathing opinion of the other, and the airing of their quarrel was diminishing public respect for the administration's recovery program.

President Roosevelt, with the aim of bringing N.R.A. into line with a broader program for economic recovery, appointed the Industrial Emergency Committee. This was a small group, including only the heads of the agencies concerned, and was authorized, "To make recommendations to the President . . . with respect to problems of relief, public works, labor disputes and industrial recovery, together with allied problems of agricultural recovery . . . and to determine, with the approval of the President, the general policies of the administration of the National Industrial Recovery Act." [9]

As matters turned out, the Industrial Emergency Committee was unable to formulate an acceptable policy. It may be that informal conference is more useful than an interdepartmental committee in resolving a serious dispute between administrative officials.[10] Nevertheless, interdepartmental committees have

9 Executive Order 6859, September 27, 1934. See p. 122 below.

10 It may be that neither an informal conference nor an interdepartmental committee will succeed in resolving an important conflict among high administrative officials unless the President is prepared to intervene. In such situations, however, an interdepartmental committee should not be appointed as

repeatedly been established with the hope of easing situations highly charged with controversy.

Third, when more than two departments are involved and the problem seems to be a continuing one, and at the same time it does not seem desirable to concentrate the activity in a single agency, an interdepartmental committee has often been considered more satisfactory than an informal arrangement. This broad description accounts for the establishment of the great majority of interdepartmental committees. Many times there has been no definite reason for setting up the committee. It just seemed at the time to be a good idea. For example, the Transportation Legislation Committee, Secretary Roper's Advisory Committee on Transportation, the Business Advisory Council's committees on transportation, safety at sea, and air transport, the Shipping Policy Committee, and a number of additional minor groups were all appointed in 1934 with the vague task of studying interdepartmental aspects of federal transportation problems. One well-planned committee would have been more effective than the combined efforts of these groups ultimately proved to be.

On the other hand, many committees of this third type have been set up with care, given a definite function, and started on a well-planned program. The Interdepartment Radio Advisory Committee is an illustration in point. This committee had its origin in the First National Radio Conference, called by Secre-

a coordinating agency. When interdepartmental consultation is required in a problem in which only the President can make the final decision, nothing more than research should be expected from the interdepartmental group. The idea of imposing pressure from above to achieve agreement in an interdepartmental committee seems to be a contradiction in terms. Unless officials are prepared, even determined, to cooperate, it is futile to bring them together in an interdepartmental committee. Moreover, when it is known that the President is willing to interpose, the tendency is for an administrator to try in private conversation to bring the President around to his point of view. Nevertheless, a negative sort of pressure from above, a deliberate notification of a hands-off attitude on the part of the higher authority, has sometimes seemed to encourage agreement among the members of an interdepartment committee. See pp. 140 and 145 below.

tary of Commerce Herbert Hoover in the spring of 1922. With a view to finding a means for making the maximum effective use of the wavelengths available for government broadcasting, and insuring proper representation to all the departments concerned, Dr. S. W. Stratton, chairman of the conference, suggested to the Secretary of Commerce that the interested departments be invited to designate representatives on a government committee for this purpose. Representatives were named, and the committee met during the recess of the conference. Among its recommendations was one for the establishment of a permanent interdepartmental advisory committee on radio broadcasting by government departments, which was approved by the Secretary. The committee was set up by letter of the Secretary of Commerce to ten departments and agencies, inviting each to participate. In December, 1922, the committee suggested to the Secretary of Commerce that its functions be extended to include non-radio matters covering all forms of electrical communication. Since the Radio Act of 1927, the main function of the committee has been the allocation of radio frequencies to government stations. Broadcasting frequencies in general are assigned by two authorities, the President, who assigns those used by government stations, and the Federal Communications Commission, which assigns all others. Since 1927, when President Coolidge requested the Secretary of Commerce to coordinate the allocation of governmental radio frequencies, this presidential task has been delegated to the Interdepartment Radio Advisory Committee.

The second major step in setting up an interdepartmental committee is the selection of the individuals who are to serve on it. At the core of the personnel problem in the interdepartmental committee are two desiderata, somewhat in conflict. The first is knowledge, the second, power. There is need, in the process of interdepartmental coordination, for the sort of knowledge that can come only from great familiarity with the details of departmental operations. Every problem confronting the committee will be expressed in terms of a specific situation.

Every such situation will arise from specialized operations. Consequently, the discussions must always be based upon specialized knowledge. This fact accounts for the presence of bureau chiefs in the membership of so many interdepartmental committees. In most cases, they are the officials who have the requisite knowledge. But effective coordination also requires that the official serving on the committee have the power of decision. Unfortunately, the two characteristics are seldom combined in a single individual. An exception to the rule is Secretary of Agriculture Wallace, whose presence on the Executive Committee on Commercial Policy means that agricultural problems can be given authoritative interpretation in the group's discussions. In general, however, it must be assumed that the combination of knowledge and power will have to be sought in a combination of different levels of officials.

Five kinds of officials have been used in interdepartmental committees: the heads of executive agencies, assistant secretaries, administrative assistants and personal advisers, bureau chiefs, and career administrators below the rank of bureau chief. How can one judge the value of the contribution which officials of various ranks are able to make in the coordinating process? Clearly, there can be no objective test. The success of each committee depends on a large number of factors, and no two examples are exactly comparable. We can, however, draw some conclusions from the performance of each type of official, first in those committees where all members are of the same rank, and second, the relative usefulness of each level in committees where they have been mixed. Between 1932 and 1936, there have been in existence at least 27 important committees which have included Cabinet officials or heads of independent agencies. Of this number, 15 committees contained no officials of lower rank, though in most cases they used a secretariat composed of permanent officials. Assistant secretaries have been used in a total of 15 committees, five of which were made up exclusively of such officials—again with subcommittees or secretariats using career administrators. Bureau chiefs participated in 33 committees, but no committee used this type of official alone. In 11 committees permanent officials of lower rank than bureau chief comprised the entire membership. These figures suggest that the contribution of the permanent official has at least seemed as necessary to the coordinating process as that of the political official.

In order to make an effective contribution to an interdepartmental committee, an official, regardless of his rank, must have a reasonably large amount of time to spend on this work. He must not be overburdened with departmental responsibilities. When one examines the attendance records of various committees, it appears that the assistant secretaries and the personal assistants to the department head are best able to devote a relatively great amount of time to interdepartmental contacts.[11] For example, in the course of the 26 meetings held by the Special Industrial Recovery Board, eight Cabinet officials, four assistant secretaries, and one assistant to the Secretary attended as regular members. Of the eight department heads, the chairman missed only two meetings, but the other seven averaged only 13 meetings or attendance half the time. The highest attendance record was 21 meetings, the lowest only 5. The four assistant secretaries, however, had an average attendance of 18 meetings, with the highest record of attendance 23 meetings and the lowest 12. Turner Battle, Assistant to the Secretary of Labor, was the only official of this rank to attend as a regular member of the committee; he was present at 17 meetings. However, at least five other personal aides or administrative assistants attended meetings at various times. Another example of a committee including several types of officials in its membership was the Special Board for Public Works. This group held 25 meetings in all, attended regularly by five Cabinet officials, five assistant secretaries, two assistants to department heads,

11 The figures cited here are not meant to be conclusive, but only suggestive. It is impossible to make tables of attendance records covering a great number of committeees, for record-keeping has not been uniform and data are available in only a few cases.

and ten permanent administrators of varying grades. Of the Cabinet secretaries, the chairman missed only two meetings, but the other four averaged an attendance of only six meetings, or a quarter of the time. The assistant secretaries appeared to spend more time on their work in this committee than either the secretaries or the non-political officials. The five assistant secretaries who were with the committee from start to finish had an average attendance record of 17 meetings, the highest 20 and the lowest four. One of the special assistants to the secretary attended 21 meetings, the other 17. The seven permanent administrators who were with the committee all through averaged an attendance of 15 meetings, the highest 24 and the lowest four.

It is not easy to estimate the range of the official's knowledge of departmental operations. He must have either specialized knowledge of a particular activity within his own department, or specialized knowledge of some aspect of the particular problem confronting the interdepartmental group to which he is appointed. This does not, of course, exclude the rare individual who happens in addition to have a broad familiarity with all the procedures of his own or other agencies. But any generalization regarding the effectiveness of each type of official must be carefully qualified. The considerations which have initially dictated the appointment to office of Cabinet members are not such as would lead one to look to them for specialized knowledge of a particular field of administration. As a rule, committees composed of Cabinet officials have not been successful integrating devices unless their discussions were supplemented by creative staff work. The members of the Central Statistical Committee are hard to assemble, and there is every reason to believe that the discussions of this group are perfunctory. The minutes of the Special Industrial Recovery Board and the Special Board for Public Works suggest that the Cabinet members were usually unable to discuss their own departments' problems in concrete terms unless primed by their subordinates. As a rule, the permanent administrators spoke for their chiefs in these meetings. Otherwise, no question could be raised that had not been on the advance agenda. On the other hand, Secretary of Agriculture Wallace has been an outstanding figure in every committee on which he has served. He has always been able to contribute concrete information and an intelligent viewpoint; in addition he has frequently raised questions of the widest import, attempting to explore the long-run significance of the issues discussed. Secretary of Labor Perkins has also possessed specific knowledge of departmental detail, and has often tried to raise the level of committee discussions to consideration of general problems and policies. Secretary of the Treasury Morgenthau is a third exceptional case, especially in committees where his department assumed leadership in coordination, as in the Loan Committee.[12]

A revealing illustration of the role of the department head in an interdepartmental committee is afforded by the Industrial Emergency Committee.[13] This committee had every facility for successful coordination of high policy. It was a small group, easily manageable in discussion. It was given a clear mandate and well-defined terms of reference. All members were of equal rank, and there was no suggestion of coercive or steamroller tactics. Meetings were held in one of the White House council rooms, so that the committee could always give the President the results of its discussions without delay. Under these circumstances, the group managed to work out half a dozen policies on problems of major importance. It is noteworthy that they never took an unfinished argument to the President, but always a decision. Naturally, these policies were compromises, not wholly satisfactory to anyone. In most instances, after the committee had reached a conclusion and received the President's approval of the decision, the individual department heads would simply neglect to enforce it in their own organizations. For example,

12 See p. 138 below.

13 The Industrial Emergency Committee was set up by Executive Order 6859, September 27, 1934. See p. 115 above.

the committee evolved a work relief policy based on the idea of a subsistence payment to relief workers amounting to government insurance of people on relief. According to this proposal, a man on relief was to be guaranteed a minimum subsistence payment; then, if he were offered a job on one of the works programs he would be obliged to take it or go off relief rolls. If the job paid less than his relief payment, he would receive the differential from the relief agency. If it paid more, but had no assurance of permanence, he would be assured of his subsistence payment when the job stopped. In any case, he would not be dropped from the relief rolls. The same principle applied to jobs in private employment. In a word, these people were to be " insured reliefers ". Only if they received a job in private employment which was a truly permanent job would they be removed from the relief rolls. It is not the province of this chapter to appraise the merits of this plan. The point is that it was an administrative policy agreed on by direct discussion around the White House conference table. The participants were Mr. Hopkins, Mr. Ickes, Mr. Chester Davis, Mr. Clay Williams, Mr. Arthur Altmeyer or Mr. Isador Lubin acting as alternates for Secretary Perkins, and Mr. Donald Richberg as Director of the committee. The discussions were, on the whole, quiet and reasonable. But the policy was a compromise. The prevailing wage problem was still essentially unsolved, and the pressure of labor groups on Miss Perkins and on Mr. Ickes as head of P.W.A. meant that certain elements were more or less irreconcilable. Consequently the policy never became really effective, for it was never applied in the participating agencies.

The magnum opus of the Industrial Emergency Committee was its report to the President on the fundamental policies of the reorganized N.R.A. Though this has merely historical interest now, it may be cited as the probable optimum in policy-coordination by a committee composed of heavily burdened heads of agencies. The committee's nine recommendations were as follows:

(1) A permanent law providing for adoption of codes of fair competition for trades and industries engaged in interstate commerce, or which, in their operation, may seriously affect or burden interstate commerce.

(2) Establishment of codes to eliminate child labor, fix minimum wages, standards, maximum hours, etc. (including the rights of collective bargaining), flexibly designed to meet varying conditions of industry and changing industrial conditions.

(3) Codes to outlaw clearly unfair trade practices.

(4) Requirement, in codes, for collection of adequate statistics to provide a basis for code enforcement and continuing balance of production and consumption.

(5) Exempt cooperative activities from the anti-trust laws.

(6) Provision for emergency action to control destructive price cutting or over-production if it threatens to destroy fair competitive conditions and break down labor standards.

(7) Establish administrative agency for approval, revision, and voluntary enforcement of codes.

(8) Separation of governmental powers of compulsory enforcement of code requirements from the code administering agency.

(9) Legislative determination of penalties for violation of law or code.

The Industrial Emergency Committee has been the only committee of its kind. No other interdepartmental group has functioned without staff aid from permanent officials. Consequently, it is of considerable significance that this group was unable to get its decisions enforced by the agencies concerned. These policies were matters of prime importance. Had a group of bureau chiefs failed in achieving agreement on them, there would have seemed to be ground for saying that the authority of the department head was essential to effective coordination in an interdepartmental committee. It seems obvious, however, that the power which comes solely or primarily from official rank is not necessarily of great importance in the coordinating process. This conclusion is buttressed by analysis of the relatively successful operations of the Committee on Economic

Security, the Executive Committee on Commercial Policy, and those other committees that have used a group of department heads as the superstructure of a staff of permanent administrators.

The contribution of the assistant secretary may be described in much the same terms as that of the department head. Where assistant secretaries were outright patronage appointees, they contributed nothing but their time to committee meetings. Some of them, however, had special interests which made them useful for consideration of broad policies on the basis of information supplied by an executive secretariat. The Health and Welfare Committee is the outstanding example. In general, there are two principal objections to assistant secretaries for interdepartmental coordination. They are patronage appointees, usually having no knowledge of the field to which they are assigned. Moreover, they are sometimes presidential advisers, with no real interest in departmental problems nor time to spend on them.

The use, in interdepartmental committees, of administrative assistants and other aides to the department head has not been sufficiently systematic to make possible any generalization. It should be noted, however, that this type of official is singularly useful for interdepartmental contacts.[14]

14 See Arthur W. Macmahon, "Departmental Management", in *Report and Special Studies,* President's Committee on Administrative Management, p. 249 *et seq.* Regarding the group of officials (administrative assistants and aides to the department head) who constitute the core of departmental management, Professor Macmahon says: "It equips the Secretary for his relationships outside of the department, with the President and with the heads of other agencies, individually or in the Cabinet and directly or through staff representation. In these connections, it brings up to the Secretary, properly simplified and sharpened, information regarding the situations that call for discussion and decision; and when arrangements have been made, it transmits the directions that translate intentions into actions. In addition, departmental management facilitates the necessarily numerous and specialized relationships through which much of the work of coordination must be conducted. A managerial personnel in itself provides the conveniently appropriate focuses for many of the interdepartmental contacts that are involved. It can encourage such contacts at the bureau level or below, furthermore,

It must be concluded, therefore, that the furnishing of knowledge is the task of the non-political, permanent administrative official. His contribution to the interdepartmental committee is twofold, precision of factual detail on the one hand, and continuity on the other. The type of information contributed by the political official is more generalized, more amateur than professional, and important chiefly for its political or policy-making implications. The records of interdepartmental committees thoroughly support this conclusion.

Finally, a word of appraisal is necessary regarding the factor of power, the ability of an official to make a decision on the problems being considered by the committee without first consulting a higher official in his department. In estimating the ability to decide, even more than the factors of knowledge or freedom from administrative routine, it is difficult to frame objective criteria for judging the relative usefulness of different types of official in the coordinating process. The power of decision legally rests with the department head, except as it is delegated by him to his subordinates. But can it be said that the man who furnishes the crucial data on which a decision is based is not in fact the man who makes the decision? The theoretical ideal envisages an official from the permanent civil service who will sift the facts without bias and present to his political superior the possible alternatives. In American experience with interdepartmental committees there has been scarcely even an approximation of the theoretical ideal. Instead, the power of decision has been delegated and redelegated. The department head will ask an assistant secretary to " represent " him at committee meetings, with the tacit assumption that the latter is to have full authority to act for his superior. Asked by the committee for his department's decision the assistant secretary, unequipped with the necessary factual information, will hedge with the statement that he merely represents his chief and can-

without losing sight of the need for a comprehensive concert of administrative action."

not bind the department. The meeting closes inconclusively and the assistant secretary draws his bureau chiefs into the problem. They may merely supply him with data, or they may be invited to attend the next meeting of the committee. Out of the ensuing discussions a degree of coordination among the departments is usually achieved. It may be merely that the permanent administrators bring their procedures into line with those of the other departments participating. It may happen, on the other hand, that recommendations going up from the bureau chief to the assistant secretary or department head are expressed in a memorandum of instructions signed by the department head. Finally, it may be that the interdepartmental committee itself adopts a resolution which is made the basis for future action by the constituent departments. No criticism of the process of designating subordinate officials to act for the department head is implied in the foregoing description. It seems obvious, however, that the actual delegation of authority should be clarified. In other words, an essential part of the process of setting up an interdepartmental committee is to give the officials appointed to the committee full power to act for their departments.

Such tentative conclusions as can be drawn from this survey may be summarized in the statement that the activity of establishing an interdepartmental committee should concentrate upon defining the committee's function and terms of reference. The appointment of personnel should be based primarily on an appraisal of the relative fitness of the officials available, in the light of the task the committee is expected to perform. In most instances, the bureau chief or other permanent official who is most directly involved in the actual work can safely be given full authority to make decisions for his department. When matters of general policy must be discussed, the political official must be used. In such cases, where an assistant secretary has the other qualifications mentioned above, this official should find his greatest usefulness in the field of interdepartmental relations. Should the position of permanent under- or assistant secretary be developed in the American national administration, this official might become a natural focus for interdepartmental contacts.[15] The secretary, finally, will continue to be named to many more committees than he is actually expected to participate in, and will continue to make most of his decisions on the basis of " recommendations " from below. In any case, where political officials are used extensive staff work will be essential in order to give a solid foundation to the committee's discussions.

15 See A. W. Macmahon, *op. cit.*, p. 265.

CHAPTER VI

PROBLEMS OF PROCEDURE

ONCE the committee has been set up, its effectiveness depends on the ability of its members to construct procedures which will enable them to accomplish the committee's objectives. A review of the interdepartmental committee's operations will include four elements. First, there is the part played by the executive secretary and the committee staff. Second, the role of the chairman must be described and evaluated. Third, the use of subcommittees is worth noting. Finally, the problems of reporting and responsibility are of fundamental importance. Each of these phases will be described in turn.

Sometimes the committee is supported by a special congressional appropriation or an administrative allocation of funds to furnish it with an executive secretary and appropriate clerical help. More often, the committee is supplied with its staff by contributions of money or employees from the participating agencies. In the case of about a dozen committees, really extensive use has been made of an executive secretariat. That is, the work done by the staff has gone beyond the perfunctory record keeping which characterizes the great majority of committees.

The staffing of the Joint Economy Board is typical not only of those committees which coordinate the activity of the War and Navy Departments, but also of many committees in the civilian services. Such groups are so organized that the committee itself meets only infrequently, the burden of the work being carried by the permanent organization. Lieutenant-Colonel Jarvis Butler is executive secretary of the Joint Economy Board, which was established in 1933 to investigate and report to the War and Navy Departments all economies which could be affected by the elimination of overlapping or the simplification of functions in the joint operations of the two services. The key to the present scheme of organization, which was worked out by Lieutenant-Colonel Butler, is that the Joint Economy Board acts as a court of review for the work done in its secretariat. The Board meets only when its executive secretary wishes to present to it an accumulation of cases for formal action. A survey of staff and bureaus in the army and navy revealed that in 20 major activities the two services work along parallel lines. Thereupon, each of the staffs and bureaus concerned with these 20 activities appointed a man to act as liaison officer with the Joint Economy Board. In all, there are 51 such officers; they are the people who do the spade work. Each of them, keeping close touch with the work of his establishment with an eye to possible economies, confers with the corresponding officer in the other service, to work out specific economies. Such information is then sent to Lieutenant-Colonel Butler. The liaison officers have never met as a group. When problems accumulate and decisions on policy become necessary the secretary calls a meeting of the Board and presents an agenda to it. At first the Board met daily, but as the work was brought under control meetings were put on a quarterly basis. Minutes, though not in verbatim form, are kept of Board meetings and these, together with all the records and files, are kept in the office of the executive secretary.

The situation is essentially similar in two other cases, the National Advisory Committee for Aeronautics, and the Committee on Designation of Airports of Entry. The Aeronautics committee, however, has a special appropriation of about a million dollars annually, to finance its research staff of 315 employees at Langley Field, Virginia, its clerical staff of 45 people in Washington, and its two representatives in Paris. Members of the committee receive in addition the regular governmental allowance for travel while attending meetings six times a year.[1] The committee staff is headed by a director of

[1] This committee was given statutory authorization by Act of Congress approved March 3, 1915 (USC title 50, sec. 153). See the *Twenty-first Annual Report* of the National Advisory Committee for Aeronautics (Government Printing Office, Washington, 1936).

research, Mr. George W. Lewis, and the executive secretary, Mr. John F. Victory. The work of the clerical staff is divided into five sections, purchasing, personnel, correspondence, minutes and records, and mimeographing. On the research side, the Washington staff includes some draftsmen, with two engineers in the inventions section. The executive staff acts as the committee's agent in preparing research programs. A proposed problem will originate with a subcommitte (who may get the idea from various sources, mainly the army and navy), and will be referred to the committee staff for decision as to whether the research will be conducted at Langley Field or in one of the numerous private laboratories cooperating with the committee.

The Interdepartmental Committee on Designation of Airports of Entry also places heavy reliance on its secretariat. The Customs Bureau of the Treasury Department supplies the staff. Mr. Frank Dow, Assistant Commissioner, acts as executive secretary and is aided by his administrative assistant, Mr. W. N. Crymes, and a stenographer. Mr. Dow occupies a key position in the Customs service, and this work is only a small item of his activity. Operations have been so organized that the committee has not had to hold a meeting since April 26, 1934. Such contacts with members as were necessary were made by telephone or correspondence. When a city wishes to have its airport established as a port of entry, the matter is first referred by the head of the Customs Bureau to Mr. Dow, and automatically goes to Mr. Crymes for collection of data about the city and airport from the field officers of the Customs Bureau. Mr. Crymes also obtains a report on the city from the Public Health Service and the Plant Quarantine Bureau. He then sends the file around to the members of the committee for final decision on the airport. In addition, the established airports are checked at least annually by the committee staff. Most ports are established only for one year at a time.

The secretariat of the Committee on Civil International Aviation is drawn from the Protocol Division of the State

Department. Richard Southgate, Chief of the Division of International Conferences, is executive secretary, and Stephen Latchford, an official of the Treaty Division, assists him. Using the clerical help of the Protocol Division, these men prepare legal forms for the negotiations and the blanket agreements signed by the countries involved. This work is entirely within the normal range of State Department activity. It started in an informal way when Mr. Southgate was an official in the Protocol Division, but the work expanded to such an extent that a separate unit seemed necessary. Consequently, a new unit, the Division of International Conferences, was set up. At the same time, the Commerce Department has several of its men working on problems of international air commerce. Two of these are in the Solicitor's Division, concentrating on international law aspects, and their work supplements and apparently occasionally duplicates the work done in the State Department. The Commerce Department lawyers in general work only on the broad legal questions and do not lay the actual foundations for negotiations. Typical of the problems which have been considered independently by the State Department and Commerce Department units is the question whether the independent status of the Philippines makes the granting of a franchise to a Dutch corporation for an air route over the Philippines a matter of diplomacy to be handled by the United States, or a matter of commerce, to be handled by the Philippine legislature. The Bureau of Air Commerce (now merged in the Civil Aeronautics Authority) also contributes some people on a part-time basis to the staff of the committee, but the groups from the two departments have not been organized as a single unit.

In quite a different category are the committees which do not build up any staff but appoint an executive secretary with no set range of duties. In the Special Board for Public Works, Oscar Chapman, Assistant Secretary of Interior, was appointed executive secretary by Mr. Ickes, who was the committee chairman. Mr. Chapman took part in the discussions as a member of the committee and apparently had no special function. The same was true in every detail in the case of the Special Industrial Recovery Board, where John Dickinson, Assistant Secretary of Commerce, was appointed executive secretary by Chairman Roper.

In the case of the Interdepartmental Loan Committee, however, an arrangement similar to the foregoing cases turned out differently in practice.[2] Cyril B. Upham, Assistant to the Secretary of the Treasury, who was appointed executive secretary, deliberately avoided any development of a clerical staff on the one hand, but on the other hand assumed a leading role himself in the coordinating process. Mr. Upham used his own stenographer to keep practically verbatim minutes of meetings, but these were never circulated to committee members, only two copies being made. The executive secretary worked very closely with the chairman, going over every detail of the committee's work and unofficially acting as the chairman's alter ego. Subcommittee meetings were frequently held in Mr. Upham's office, and he conferred with committee members personally outside the formal meetings.

These three committees illustrate contrasting methods of using an executive secretary. The Special Industrial Recovery Board kept verbatim reports of its meetings, and distributed mimeographed copies of the minutes to all committee members. The Special Board for Public Works followed a similar practice. But the discussions of the Loan Committee, so far as the members were concerned, went unrecorded. Secretary Morgenthau was obviously too busy to give the committee more than partial attention. Consequently, the burden of achieving cooperation was put upon the executive secretary, who made extensive use of informal subcommittees for discussion of problems involving only two or three agencies. For a time the Loan Committee met regularly and often, sometimes twice a week or more. It was especially active in the fall of 1934, when

2 The Loan Committee was established by Presidential letter to the Secretary of the Treasury, November 1, 1934. See p. 193 below.

it was drafting the banking legislation of 1935. Except for a perfunctory report of the Loan Committee's major decisions to the National Emergency Council, however, the record of these conversations is locked in the bosom of the Treasury. Not even the committee members know how often it has met, or what has been discussed in its subcommittee meetings. Some members have declared the committee to be inactive, but the Treasury Department reports that it " meets frequently."

A second general factor, of equal importance with the secretariat in the effective organization of the interdepartmental committee, is the role of the chairman. Leadership can do no more than tip the scales toward effective coordination, but it can often turn a weak committee into a successful one, and can help a strong committee to do a really brilliant job.

The chairman's role is of course conditioned at the start by his own position in the administration and by the amount of authority over the committee which the chairman is given at the time of his appointment. If the chairman is himself responsible for the program, the interdepartmental committee's relationship to him will be essentially advisory. This was true, *inter alia,* of the Advisory Council for Emergency Conservation Work, where Robert Fechner, as director of the program, was *ex officio* chairman of the Council. In most cases, however, the chairman is not officially responsible for the program and the committee is advisory only in the broadest sense. Sometimes the chairman of such a group will be appointed, sometimes elected. Though it might be expected that the appointed chairman would be put in a position of some authority over the group, this has never been the case, except when the chairman was officially responsible for the program. For example, the fact that the chairman of the Central Statistical Board has a position authorized by statute may add to his prestige but gives him no real authority over his colleagues on the Board. Similarly, in the case of the Central Housing Committee Mr. Delano was appointed by the President to head the group but was given no authority to force a decision. It seems apparent, then, that the chairman's own personality has been of relatively great importance, particularly his possession of such characteristics as tact, imagination, intelligence and personal forcefulness. What various chairmen have been able to do with their committees can perhaps be seen most clearly through a few illustrations.

One of the relatively few instances in which committees have been set up as purely advisory bodies is the National Advisory Health Council. In this case the chairman occupies an *ex officio* position which is explicitly defined by the statute creating the committee. Both governmental and non-governmental experts are included in the Council, which is called together once a year by the Surgeon-General of the Public Health Service for the sole and express purpose of giving him information and advice. The Surgeon-General prepares, from information supplied by the bureaus under his jurisdiction, a list of subjects on which the Public Health Service needs information, and sends this to the members of his advisory council some weeks in advance of the date which he has set for its meeting. The Council members then assemble in his office and in a series of meetings discuss the questions raised in the light of their work during the year. The Surgeon-General may ask for advice from council members or the group may volunteer suggestions, but in no case is the Surgeon-General obligated to accept or act upon such advice or suggestions. For the most part, council meetings have been devoted to highly technical discussions of medical problems. Recently, however, there has been an effort to reappraise the role of the federal government in public health activity, and the council has discussed such broad problems as the methods of educating the public to control venereal diseases.

In the Advisory Council for Emergency Conservation Work, the committee occupies an advisory position, but the chairman necessarily places extensive reliance on it. The C.C.C. program operates through bureaus in four departments, War, Labor, Interior and Agriculture. Representatives of these departments compose the Advisory Council. Mr. Fechner, the director of the program, calls the Council together at approximately monthly intervals, when the accumulation of work requires some sort of decision. In the early days of the program when the Council was working out major policies, meetings were even more frequent. At present, meetings are devoted to discussions of operating details, fitting them into the broad outlines of policy and making such day-to-day policy decisions as whether enrollees shall be fingerprinted, and in what way a particular appropriation shall be divided among the agencies participating in the work. At the beginning, therefore, it was essential that the chairman guide the committee's discussions tactfully in order to achieve a maximum of cooperation. He has never tried to steam-roller the discussions, nor has he ever had occasion to overrule the committee's decisions. Consequently, a very satisfactory working relationship has been established. The council has been a source of information to the director, a forum for discussion among the bureau chiefs, a clearing house for all decisions so that each department knew precisely what was going on. It has been responsible to the director but its members were never coerced by him. He has been guided by its decisions yet apparently never hampered or delayed in action. A possible explanation of this phenomenon is the careful combination of authority and leadership. Responsibility for the work was put on one individual, and the interdepartmental committee was brought in at the level where it could be of genuine aid—not in a supervisory but in an advisory capacity. The chairman soft-pedalled his prestige and authority, to emphasize the importance of the council's advice. At the same time, he always kept firm control over discussions, holding them down to specific situations. Finally, the fact that the director was in close personal contact with the President has been of great importance in achieving cooperation among the bureaus participating in the C.C.C. program. Mr. Fechner went to the White House before every council meeting, and almost always referred to his talk with the President in the course of the council's discussion.

In the case of the Special Board for Public Works, again the chairman was in close personal contact with the President. This was a group of higher ranking officials, including the Secretaries of Interior (chairman), War, Commerce, and Labor, the Solicitor General, and a varying number of bureau chiefs from the Treasury, Commerce and War Departments. Mr. Ickes simply transmitted to the interdepartmental group the President's public works policy as it developed, and it was assumed that the departments would bring their procedures into conformity.

The common practice in the group of committees which coordinate the work of the army and navy is to provide that the ranking officer present shall preside. In these instances the responsibility upon the chairman is minimized. He is not a coordinating agent but merely a parliamentary figure.

The Interdepartment Radio Advisory Committee is an illustration of the successful use of an elected chairman. The meetings of this group are held at fortnightly intervals and are devoted to discussion and disposition of the requests of the departments for assignment to particular broadcasting wavelengths. The chairman is chosen largely on the basis of personal characteristics, since he is expected to act as arbiter in reconciling conflicting departmental claims to radio frequencies.

The third general element in the interdepartmental committee's operations is the use of subcommittees. Almost all committees have utilized some sort of subcommittee arrangement, though in most cases this has been so informal as to be of no significance. In general, two forms of subcommittee are found, the group made up of members from the main committee, and the group made up of officials from the same departments but generally of lower official rank than the members of the main committee. The higher the rank of the members of an interdepartmental committee, the more use it will make of subcommittees; though the exception must here again be noted of the committee which brings together a few high officials for a confidential discussion of policy, in which case no formal organization is used.

Committees which have used sub-groups drawn from the main committee fall into two categories: those which use the subcommittee for preliminary consideration of details to conserve the time of the main committee; and those which use the subcommittee as a device for dividing the membership of a committee into groups, each of which is to deal with a specialized problem or special aspect of the general problem either because of special knowledge and competence or merely for convenience. The Special Board for Public Works offers an example of the first type. This board appointed a subcommittee on federal projects, consisting of Under Secretary of Agriculture R. G. Tugwell and Turner Battle, Assistant to the Secretary of Labor, to study all works projects proposed by federal departments and to sort out those worthy of the board's consideration. In the later days of its existence, the board did little more than ratify the decisions of this subcommittee, generally without much discussion of the projects.

The Interdepartmental Loan Committee is an example of the second type, using subcommittees to divide the membership of the main committee into groups of specialists. The Loan Committee is of special interest because it was one of the very few interdepartmental committees directly charged with responsibility for legislative clearance. The plan which provided for clearance of departmental legislative requests in the 74th session of Congress specifically mentioned that amendments to the Banking Act should clear through the Loan Committee.[3] The members of this committee, in the fall of 1934, organized into several sub-groups for the purpose of coordinating the legislative proposals of the lending agencies. One sub-group

3 Budget Circular No. 336, December 1, 1935. For a description of this plan, see E. E. Witte, "The Preparation of Proposed Legislative Measures," in *Report and Special Studies,* President's Committee on Administrative Management (Washington, 1937), at p. 365.

dealt with banking legislation, another with farm credit, a third with housing proposals. In each case, the proposed bills were first drafted by the agency most directly concerned, were discussed and re-shaped by the subcommittee, and were put into final form by the legal staff of the agency or the Treasury. The subcommittee then took the proposed bills to the White House for approval, after which they were immediately taken to the appropriate congressional committee leaders.

The Loan Committee's experience with the Banking Act of 1935 will serve as an illustration of the foregoing procedure. This bill was prepared in piecemeal fashion and considered by the Loan Committee while still in segments. Part I, relating to the guarantee of bank deposits, was in the first instance worked out in the Federal Deposit Insurance Corporation. Mr. Leo Crowley, head of this agency, employed Herman L. Ekern, a former attorney-general of his state (Wisconsin) and the man who piloted both of the railroad retirement acts through Congress, to draft a bill for the FDIC providing for a permanent system of the guarantee of bank deposits. Mr. Ekern worked on this bill throughout the fall of 1934. Several conferences on the measure were called by Mr. Crowley, bringing in a considerable number of other departments. Active participants in these conferences included Mr. Marriner Eccles, then Assistant Secretary of the Treasury and soon thereafter appointed Governor of the Federal Reserve Board; Professor Jacob Viner, Special Assistant to the Secretary of the Treasury; and Mr. Winfield Riefler, then chairman of the Central Statistical Board, Economic Adviser to the National Emergency Council, and generally regarded as the President's own economist. The highly controversial Part II of the Banking Act was generally understood to represent the ideas of Mr. Eccles, and was prepared under his direction. Part III made minor amendments in the banking and federal reserve acts, and was largely drafted in the Treasury. The influence of the Loan Committee as a group was negligible. The various parts of the bill were drafted in the agencies most directly concerned, and the President himself had the final word. But the members of the Loan Committee were nearly all people who had connections with the departments concerned with the various segments of the banking bill, and it may have been useful to go through the motions of appointing a subcommittee. Interdepartmental consultation might have taken place in any event, but the Treasury Department likes to think that the Loan Committee facilitated the process. In the case of the subcommittee on housing proposals, no agreement was reached and each agency sent its own programs independently to Congress. Neither banking nor housing proposals were ever discussed by a meeting of the full committee.

As a fourth major feature of the interdepartmental committee's operations, provision is made for periodic reports of its activity. Such reports may be submitted as confidential memoranda to the official who appointed the committee, or their contents may be made public in a press release, or they may even be printed for general distribution. In any case, there is a dual purpose in requiring reports from interdepartmental committees. First, the report offers a clue to the committee's effectiveness, if only by the implicit obligation to state the committee's terms of reference and describe how it has tried to fulfill its assigned task. Second, systematic reporting makes it possible to fit the work of all interdepartmental committees into the administrative structure. By furnishing a report of its activity the committee is made answerable, directly or indirectly, to the central authority in the organization. Scrutiny of all interdepartmental committes by some central agency is desirable in order to make sure that interdepartmental coordination is applied to those problems where it is needed, and to check up from time to time on the way in which particular committees are functioning.

There has been only one attempt to coordinate the activity of interdepartmental committees by systematizing their reporting. This was in 1934, when the National Emergency Council made a special study of interdepartmental committees. In November, 1934, in a National Emergency Council meeting, the question was raised whether interdepartmental committees were not being unduly proliferated. On November 17 a memorandum was sent by the Council's executive secretary to all heads of executive departments and agencies, requesting the names of committees on which they, or representatives of their departments, were members. On December 11, 1934, the Executive Director of the Council reported the existence of 124 interdepartmental committees, boards, and commissions, which had 224 interdepartmental subcommittees, or a total of 348 separate interdepartmental units.[4] At this meeting the President appointed five assistant secretaries and a member of the NEC secretariat to a Committee on Interdepartmental Committees, charged with the task of studying the existing interdepartmental arrangements and recommending to the Council a definite policy regarding them.

The committee's report was submitted to the Council and adopted as the Council's policy on December 20, 1934. There were six parts to the policy as finally enunciated.

1. Where an interdepartmental committee functions in a purely advisory or fact-gathering capacity, then the heads of the departments or agencies concerned, to which it is advisory or for which it compiles data, should be responsible for its establishment, proper functioning, and timely abolishment (sic!).

2. Where an interdepartmental committee functions in an advisory, fact-gathering, or coordinating capacity, and in addition is authorized to make recommendations with respect to activity, the policy for which has been determined, then the head of one of the Executive Departments, or if appropriate the head of a permanent independent establishment, should be responsible.

3. When deemed necessary, information as to the activity of this second type of committee should be contained in the department head's regular bi-weekly report to the NEC.

4 By "interdepartmental subcommittees" is meant subcommittees composed of officials who are not members of the parent committee. In effect, such sub-groups are new interdepartmental committees.

4. Where an interdepartmental committee functions in an advisory, fact-gathering, or coordinating capacity, and in addition is authorized to make recommendations to the President with respect to activity, the policy for which has not been determined, the NEC should be the agency for its establishment, proper functioning and timely abolishment.

Information as to the activity of this type of committee should be contained in a report to the NEC made by the department head who is committee chairman or whose subordinate is chairman, either periodically or specially as directed by the President.

5. The establishment, proper functioning, and timely abolishment of subcommittees should be the responsibility of the parent interdepartmental committee.

6. That in the future the establishment, functions, and abolition of all interdepartmental committees as above be promptly reported to the office of the NEC.

On January 24, 1935, this policy was formally put into effect by a memorandum from the Executive Director to the heads of departments and independent agencies, announcing the action of the Council.

On the whole, this statement of policy was received by the departments without question or comment. In a few cases committees were suspicious or openly hostile toward the attempt at coordination. Thus the Secretary of Labor on January 3, 1935 wrote to the Director of the NEC that the Cabinet Committee on Prices, of which she was chairman, had no objection to reporting through the Council to the President. Secretary Perkins added, however: "The committee understands that the acceptance of your suggestion does not in any way affect its status. It was appointed by the President after the matter of prices and their fluctuation had become an important issue (*i. e.*, with reference to operation of the price provisions in the N.R.A. codes). A great deal of time, thought, and money has been expended on this activity and the Committee naturally expects to continue and complete its work." [5]

5 The Cabinet Committee on Prices sponsored the publication of *Price*

The Civil Service Commission flatly refused to have its Council of Personnel Administration act as a subcommittee of the NEC and as such report to the Council rather than to the Commission. Chairman Mitchell was told that the purpose of this proposed arrangement was merely to relieve the President of work and to have information available, should the President request it, regarding the status or amount of work completed by this group just as with any other interdepartmental committee. He replied that he understood perfectly and did not object in principle, but that the Commission felt that according to statute it was the advisory body to the President on personnel administration, and that the Council on Personnel Administration should therefore be responsible to the Commission. These two illustrations indicate that, even though they approved of the principle of coordination, those committees which already had the entrée to the White House had no intention of surrendering it.

Most of the committees, however, accepted the policy of the National Emergency Council and complied with the new procedure at least to the extent of sending the Director periodic summaries of their activity. The Interdepartmental Loan Committee, for example, sent to the NEC over a period of three months seven memoranda outlining the subject matter of the Loan Committee's work. These reports were not really descriptive of the work the committee was doing and were eventually discontinued. The NEC was under the impression that when the reports stopped the committee had disbanded, but the Treasury was in fact still using the Loan Committee.

The effort at coordination by the National Emergency Council soon became perfunctory. Finally the Council abandoned even its practice of sending weekly reminders to interdepartmental committees or requesting their reports or even keeping files on them.

and Price Policies, by Walton Hamilton and five associates (McGraw-Hill Book Company, New York, 1936). For a brief description of the Cabinet Committee, see *op. cit.*, Preface, pp. vii ff.

Although the National Emergency Council's attempt at coordination of interdepartmental committees did not succeed in practice, the statement of policy is significant for the formulation of objectives which it represents. The National Emergency Council attempted to reduce the demands on the President's time. It also attempted to clarify the lines of responsibility between interdepartmental committees and the administration heads. The fact that the Council was unable to impose its will on the constituent departments was a reflection of the inadequacy of the Council itself as a coordinating agency.

At present, therefore, the reporting activities of interdepartmental committees continue haphazard. Typical of the committees which report direct to Congress are the Foreign Service Buildings Commission, the National Archives Council, and the National Park Trust Fund Board. The Foreign Service Buildings Commission issued only one annual report, in January, 1929, but this practice was found to be too expensive for repetition. The other two groups have only recently been established and have as yet issued no formal report, but will also make a routine annual report to Congress. In two of these cases, the Foreign Service Buildings Commission and the National Archives Council, members of Congress are included in the personnel of the interdepartmental committee. The practice has invariably been to make such committees responsible directly to Congress.

During the period 1933-37, a limited number of committees made formal written reports to the President. Typical examples were the National Resources Committee, the Power Policy Committee, the Committee on Economic Security, the committee set up to study the problem of securities exchange regulation, a committee on federal incorporation, the Interdepartmental Committee on Shipping Policy, and the Central Statistical Board. In each of these cases, the report was given to the press or printed for general circulation.

Several important committees have maintained direct contact with the President. Usually this has been due to President

Roosevelt's personal interest in the work of the committee. Thus the Advisory Council for Emergency Conservation Work has been in constant contact with the White House through Director Fechner. Another example is the Industrial Emergency Committee; this group met in the White House and adjourned to report the results of discussions direct to the President. The Interdepartmental Committee on Health and Welfare, and the Central Housing Committee submitted confidential memoranda to the President in lieu of printed reports.

The Interdepartment Radio Advisory Council also reports to the President, but under somewhat different circumstances from the foregoing examples. Charged by law with the responsibility for assigning broadcasting frequencies to government radio stations, the President actually takes no part in the process of allocating frequencies except to sign the Executive Orders in which the announcement is made of new wave lengths assigned to government departments. The Executive Orders are completely prepared by the Radio Committee and are transmitted intact to the White House by the chairman of the Federal Communications Commission. The Communications Commission makes no review or revision of the interdepartmental committee's decisions, and the latter group has direct access to the President if it so desires. Two factors make such a situation possible, the technical nature of the committee's work and the fact that it has never become identified with policy-making functions in regard to radio broadcasting. Should it ever make any serious demands upon the President's time it would doubtless be made responsible to the Communications Commission.

It is clear from this review of the committees which report directly to the President that the demands upon his attention are needlessly numerous. In only one type of situation is direct contact justified—where a decision is required which can be made only by the President. Even then there seems to be no necessity for allowing interdepartmental committees to have unchallenged access to the White House. Clearance through the presidential secretariat, which is not now done even for purposes of record, might well be made a reality to the mutual benefit both of the President and the interdepartmental group.

The great majority of interdepartmental committees are at least nominally responsible to one or another of the executive departments. The interdepartmental structure which handles the Trade Agreements program is clearly a part of the State Department. It was so designated in the first letter which the President wrote on this subject. Although President Roosevelt has undoubtedly talked over various features of this work with the Secretaries of Agriculture and Commerce, it is to the State Department, to Secretary Hull and Assistant Secretary Sayre, that he looks for responsible reports on the program. No report, in the formal sense, has ever been prepared. The trade agreements with various countries are the committees' evidence of achievement, and the progress of the work is indicated by periodic mention of it in the weekly State Department *Press Releases*. Within the interdepartmental structure, of course, certain committees are charged with the duty of preparing special reports on particular subjects for submission to the higher committees, but the Trade Agreements Committee itself is responsible to the Secretary of State. In general, the characteristic situation in which the interdepartmental committee is made responsible to a department head is essentially the situation described in paragraphs 1 and 2 of the NEC statement of policy quoted above: that is, where the committee's authority is advisory and where the problem under consideration is of such importance to the particular department that the committee's report will be made an integral part of departmental policy and action.

It should be clear from this review that the term "responsibility", as applied to interdepartmental committees, need carry no connotation of a superior authority demanding at intervals that the committee's work be done according to some prearranged plan. There is needed only an adequate clearing mechanism. Most committees earnestly want a channel of communication with the administration leaders, in order to receive tentative approval on progress, an answer to the problems that inevitably arise, and an authoritative word for the future. The problem is to make certain that the interdepartmental group does not carry its current disagreements to the White House, for then the machinery created to avoid duplication of effort and to systematize interdepartmental contacts becomes clogged.

Three conclusions seem inescapable. In the first place, collective responsibility of the interdepartmental group is by no means always a necessity. There is no particular virtue in drafting memoranda for submission once a week to some central agency. The effects of responsibility can just as well be reflected in the acceptance of the committee's work by individual action of the agencies concerned. In the second place, although ultimate responsibility rests with the President, his control cannot be direct and immediate. The executive offices should be the last in a series of screens through which, as through a graded mesh, interdepartmental problems will be eliminated by prior handling. In the third place, the experience of the first Roosevelt administration with interdepartmental committees indicates the desirability of reducing the number of intermediate contacts between committee and President to a minimum.

CHAPTER VII

THE CONDITIONS OF UTILITY OF INTERDEPARTMENTAL COMMITTEES

A concluding chapter may appropriately begin with recapitulation, for the purpose of accenting certain recommendations that have been implicit in the foregoing chapters. The summary will consider first the principal types of activity for which the interdepartmental committee has been found useful, and second the essential features of successful committee organization.

Analysis has shown that interdepartmental committees are useful for five kinds of administrative endeavor. The first is the exploration and drafting of legislative proposals. The task of reconciling the legislative requests of various departments is not easy. Moreover, it is necessary to consider the larger problem of harmonizing the policies of the administration as a whole, in which not only the immediate legislative proposals but also their implications and long-run effects must be taken into account. Here is the shadowline of coordination, the border area in which an activity cannot be unmistakably identified with either the ends or the means of governmental action. The integration and planning of legislative requests is an activity which facilitates the conduct of governmental functions; it offers a means by which governmental objectives can be more clearly formulated and therefore more satisfactorily put into practice. At the same time, legislative requests are so intimately concerned with the objectives of governmental action that the task of fitting them harmoniously together in a far-seeing plan is more than mere administrative housekeeping.

The use of interdepartmental committees for coordination and planning of legislative requests is still in the experimental stage. There is not sufficient data to warrant generalization about the success or failure of the interdepartmental committee in this work. Six such groups were active between 1932 and 1936.[1] The Committee on Economic Security can tentatively be judged a success, although a definite verdict cannot be rendered until the Social Security Act has seen many years of operation. Other committees were not so felicitous. The Transportation Legislation Committee and the Shipping Policy Committee were clearly unsuccessful. In the six committees charged with integration of legislative requests, personal factors—the fitness for the assigned task of persons appointed to the committee—seem to have turned the balance between relative success or failure. As a piece of administrative machinery, the Committee on Economic Security was satisfactory. It was intelligently constructed. The quality of appointments at all levels was high. Consequently, the Committee on Economic Security may well serve as the prototype for future interdepartmental committees seeking to integrate legislative requests.

The second activity for which committees have been used is research. Between 1932 and 1936, at least 38 separate interdepartmental groups were engaged in this type of work.[2] A few

1 These six committees were:

The Committee on Economic Security.

Transportation Legislation Committee.

Shipping Policy Committee.

Interdepartmental Ocean-Mail Contract Committee.

Interdepartmental Committee on Stock Exchange Regulation.

Farm Tenancy Committee.

2 The following list covers most of the important committees, but does not pretend to be exhaustive. Research committees are continually being appointed and disbanded, and departments have not been particularly interested in keeping records of these groups once their task has been accomplished.

Cabinet Committee to Review the Nationality Laws.

  Advisory Committee to the Cabinet Committee to Review the Nationality Laws.

Interdepartmental Committee on Copyright.

Cabinet Committee to Study Prices.

  Technical Subcommittee to the Cabinet Committee on Prices.

National Advisory Health Council.

National Resources Committee.

  Planning Committee on Mineral Policy of N.R.C.

of these committees are more or less permanent agencies, notably the National Resources Committee and the National Advisory Council on Aeronautics. As a rule, however, they have been *ad hoc* bodies, set up to perform a specific task, disbanding when their report has been made. In some cases, the work of research committees has led to the framing of legislative requests. More often, however, legislation has not been directly contemplated. The committee has been given a broad

- Water Planning Section of Central Technical Committee.
- Land Planning Section.
- Industrial Resources Section.

National Power Policy Committee.

- Subcommittee on Unification of National Power Supply.
- Subcommittee on Holding Companies.
- Subcommittee on Hydro-electric.
- Subcommittee on Rural Electrification.
- Subcommittee on Cooperation with States.
- Subcommittee on Standardization of the National Rate Structure.
- Subcommittee on Government Purchase of Power.

Interdepartmental Board on Great Lakes and St. Lawrence River Project.

Mississippi River Commission.

National Forest Reservation Committee.

- Committee on Forest Practices of National Forest Reservation Committee.
- Committee to Cooperate with the Upper Monongahela Valley Planning Council.

Textile Foundation Inc.

- Flax Committee of Textile Foundation.

Committee to study a report of the Secretary of Agriculture regarding means to increase industrial employment by coordination of price and production policies in industries of vertical series, as housing and automobiles.

Occupational Research Studies Committee.

Commerce Research Committee of the Executive Board of NRA.

Committee on Federal Incorporation.

Committee on Increase in Production and Employment.

Committee to Consider Tonnage Tax.

Board of Life Saving Appliances.

National Advisory Committee for Aeronautics.

National Research Council.

Committee on Oil Pollution of Navigable Waters.

Communications Coordinating Committee.

Interdepartmental Committee on Prohibition Repeal.

mandate for general investigation, without the specific injunction to present a draft bill as part of its recommendations. Some committees of this type have been set up by the President, as the Cabinet Committee to Review the Nationality Laws, and the Committee on Federal Incorporation. The Cabinet Committee on Prices is noteworthy because it is one of the few committees known to have been appointed by the President as a result of Cabinet discussions. A few were appointed by the National Emergency Council when it was in existence. Most of the others have been created by the heads of executive agencies, as was the Interdepartmental Committee on Prohibition Repeal, set up at the instigation of the Secretary of the Treasury. Those committees which have drawn their authority from acts of Congress have usually been set up in the first instance by the President or by joint action of department heads. On the whole, research committees have been very useful. They have been an important part of the Administration's machinery for thinking. Any attempts in the future to organize a service of intelligence, a civil general staff, will necessarily involve an intensive use of research committees.

In the third type of activity, the interdepartmental committee has facilitated the conduct of an administrative program for which a single agency is definitely responsible but which has certain interdepartmental aspects. At least 45 interdepartmental groups come under this heading.[3] In many cases, such as the

3 Committees of this type are as follows:

Executive Committee on Commercial Policy.
Committee for Reciprocity Information.
Trade Agreements Committee.
  Committee on General Surveys of Trade Agreements Committee.
    Subcommittee on Transportation.
  Committee on Import Quotas.
  Branch Factories Committee.
  Committee on Exchange Control.
  Interdepartmental Country Committees.
  Interdepartmental Commodity Committees.
Foreign Trade Zones Board.
  Interdepartmental Committee of Alternates on Foreign Trade Zones.

Executive Committee on Commercial Policy and the Trade Agreements Committees, the importance of the advice given by the participating departments has been so great that the program has seemed almost independent of the agency which has been primarily responsible for it. Sometimes, indeed, the committee has become practically a separate agency. The Foreign Trade Zones Board, and the Migratory Bird Conservation Commission are two that have shown tendencies in this direction. Such an occurrence is usually unfortunate, for the committee loses sight of its original task of advising a single department, and the number of independent agencies increases.

Immigration Quota Committee.
  Subcommittee on Immigration Quotas.
Commission Created by the Grain Futures Act.
Regulatory Committee on Enforcement of the Pure Food and Drug Act.
Advisory Council for Government of the Virgin Islands.
Interdepartmental Committee on the Territory of Alaska.
Quetico-Superior Committee.
Migratory Bird Conservation Commission.
Committee to Cooperate with the Subsistence Homesteads Division.
Federal Committee on Apprentice Training.
Committee on Standards for Safety and Health under NRA Mining Codes.
Committee on Railroad Fixed Charges.
Special Board for Public Works.
Interdepartmental Ice Patrol Board.
Advisory Council to the Director of the Emergency Conservation Work.
  Advisory Committee on Education in CCC Camps.
National Archives Council.
National Historical Publications Commission.
National Capital Park and Planning Commission.
  Coordinating Committee of Above.
Federal Surplus Commodities Corporation.
National Park Trust Fund Board.
Special Board for Industrial Recovery.
Federal Business Associations.
Federal Contract Board.
Federal Standard Stock Catalog Board.
Federal Specifications Board.
Interdepartmental Subcommittees of Specifications Board.
Committee on Paper Specifications.
Interdepartmental Committee on Envelopes.

Thus the principal purpose of the interdepartmental committee as a coordinating instrument is defeated.

The fourth activity is the collegial conduct of an administrative program by the committee itself. This does not necessarily mean that the committee is set up as a new, independent agency. To be sure, this has sometimes happened, as with those government corporations which have had interdepartmental directorates.[4] More often, however, the program contemplated does not fit perfectly into any existing organization and requires the combined action of several. An interdepartmental committee is used to draw together representatives from the agencies concerned, to plan the new program and frame its policies on a cooperative basis, while the details are carried out by the various organizations separately. A total of 57 committees have fallen within this classification.[5] In using an interdepartmental com-

4 As, for example, Textile Foundation, Inc., of which the Secretaries of Commerce and Agriculture are directors; Tennessee Valley Associated Cooperatives, Inc., of which officials of Works Progress Administration and the Department of Agriculture are directors; and the Export-Import Bank of Washington, of which officials of Reconstruction Finance Corporation, and of the Commerce, State, and Treasury Departments are trustees.

5 The titles of these groups are as follows:

Interdepartmental Committee on Civil International Aviation.
Pan-American Commercial Conference Committee.
Drought Committee of 1934.
Drought Committee of 1936.
  Interdepartmental Committee on Transportation, of Drought Committee of 1936.
  Drought Planning Committee.
  Livestock Food Committee.
Puerto Rican Hurricane Relief Committee.
  Puerto Rican Rehabilitation Committee.
Federal Bureau of Hospitalization.
Deposit Liquidation Board.
Joint Merchant Vessel Board.
Interdepartmental Committee on Airports of Entry.
Patents and Designs Board.
Aeronautical Board.
U. S. Council of National Defense.
Joint Board, Army and Navy.

mittee for the actual conduct of an administrative program, there has been a tendency to overlook the real objectives of coordination. This does not mean that the committees listed above have not performed a useful function. Sometimes, how-

Joint Economy Board, Army and Navy.
Joint Board in connection with Army-Navy Communications.
Joint Army-Navy Board on Gun Forgings.
Joint Army-Navy Board on Smokeless Powder.
Joint Army-Navy Board on Ammunition Storage.
Joint Army-Navy Selective Service Committee.
The Codification Board (for Federal Register).
Arlington Memorial Amphitheater Commission.
Federal Board of Surveys and Maps.
Commodity Credit Corporation.
Export-Import Bank of Washington.
Federal Farm Mortgage Corporations.
Public Works Emergency Housing Corporation.
Interdepartmental Committee on Health and Welfare.
Advisory Committee on Allotments.
Public Health Board.
Central Statistical Board.
Army-Navy Aircraft Standards Committee.
Board of Weather Survey.
Interdepartment Radio Advisory Committee.
Aviation Procurement Committee.
Army-Navy Munitions Board.
  Commodity Committees of Army-Navy Munitions Board.
  Standardization and Specification Division.
  Price Control Division.
  Labor Division.
  Legal and Contracts Division.
  Power Division.
  Transportation Division.
  Facilities Division.
Council of Personnel Administration.
Federal Fire Council.
  Committee on Inspection and Interdepartmental Cooperation.
  Fire Record Committee.
  Fire Hazard Committee.
  Apparatus and Devices Committee.
National Archives Council.
Foreign Service Buildings Commission.
Joint Treasury-Post Office Committee on Public Buildings.
Legal Committees.

ever, the action could advantageously have been concentrated in a single agency. For example, leadership in the Drought Committees was informally taken by the Department of Agriculture. Progress might have been more satisfactory if the Department of Agriculture had been given definite responsibility from the first.

Even more serious is the susceptibility of committees engaged in the collegial conduct of a program toward duplication of work done elsewhere in the government. Thus the committees which coordinate the defense departments are perhaps unduly proliferated. For example, the Aeronautical Board, the Army-Navy Aircraft Standards Committee, and the Aviation Procurement Committee all deal with essentially the same subject matter. Moreover, the scope of their work closely resembles that done by the Joint Economy Board, which with its various subcommittees coordinates the general purchasing activity of the army and navy. In fairness it must be said at the outset that much of this work is controlled by one man, Lieutenant-Colonel Jarvis Butler, who acts as executive secretary of several of the army-navy committees, and who has worked out an excellent organization. A still greater degree of consolidation could be achieved. There is essentially no reason why the bulk of peacetime army and navy purchasing could not be handled through the Procurement Division of the Treasury. The present army-navy purchasing committees could be drawn in on an advisory basis with no loss of efficiency. Of course this will be categorically denied by the defense departments, just as central purchasing was resisted by the other executive agencies for many years, on the grounds of special technical requirements. In housekeeping activities, such as purchasing, there should be a special effort to avoid duplication of function among interdepartmental committees. The reason, aside from considerations of pure efficiency, is that committees concerned with administrative housekeeping must inevitably build up a permanent staff. Over a period of years, questions of prestige arise which make reorganization and consolidation almost impossible.

Finally, there is an unfortunate drift toward irresponsibility in this fourth type of interdepartmental committee. Because no single agency is effectively responsible for the program, no one pays much attention to what the committee is doing. Moreover, there is no central agency to supervise the work of all interdepartmental committees. Under such circumstances, the work of committees conducting an administrative program is seldom as efficient as it might be.

On the other side of the picture, there are many instances in which this fourth type of committee has been used with conspicuous success. The Interdepartmental Committee on Health and Welfare is one example.[6] The Central Statistical Board is another.[7] All the committees used to coordinate housekeeping activities fall within this classification, and most of them have been reasonably satisfactory as coordinating devices.

In general, it may be said that an interdepartmental committee is useful for directing an administrative program under two sets of circumstances. First, when it is expected that the program will be temporary and that the committee will ultimately be disbanded. Second, when the activity is intended to be permanent but the interdepartmental committee is expected to develop the nucleus of a new agency, which will either be absorbed into an existing executive department or set up as a separate department. This does not mean that the committee can be absorbed into an existing department so completely that the interdepartmental phases of the program will disappear. Interdepartmental consultation will usually continue to be a necessity. The interdepartmental committee, however, will suffer no loss in effectiveness if it is made answerable primarily to one executive agency.

The fifth use to which the interdepartmental committee has been put is the exchange or " clearing " of information, in cases where several departments are engaged in similar or related

6 See p. 70 above.

7 See p. 94 above.

activities. Seven committees conform to this pattern.[8] The classification is admittedly a tenuous one. In no case has a committee been brought into existence with the sole or express purpose of exchanging information in committee meetings. At the same time, every interdepartmental committee has recognized this as part of its task. The Central Housing Committee was set up merely to " coordinate ", with no clearer definition of its assignment. The Power Policy Committee was, at least in part, a research and discussion group. The Loan Committee was specifically authorized, among other duties, to clear certain types of legislative proposals. Unfortunately, no committee within this classification has been a sufficiently satisfactory discussion group to serve as a model. Nevertheless, there is a real need for the sort of interdepartmental committee that will serve primarily as a forum for discussion of common problems. Committees of this sort will necessarily place heavy reliance on an executive secretariat; lack of adequate staffing has hitherto been the most conspicuous defect of interdepartmental discussion groups.

These five kinds of objectives, or uses to which the interdepartmental committee has been put, are not meant to be rigid categories. Many of the committees fall within two or more classifications. The Loan Committee had the general function of coordinating the policies of the lending agencies, and also the specific tasks of clearing their legislative proposals and integrating the timing of loans with Treasury policies. Many other committees have been borderline cases. The Interdepartmental Committee on Civil International Aviation began as an independent group but is gradually coming within the

8 These committees are as follows:
Central Housing Committee.
Industrial Emergency Committee.
Power Policy Committee of 1936.
Loan Committee.
Special Committee on Government Borrowing.
Committee to Coordinate Activities Affecting Banks.
Preferred Stock Committee.

jurisdiction of the State Department. It must therefore be emphasized that these categories are no more than a convenient device for analyzing the interdepartmental committee.

Having summarized the principal objectives of the interdepartmental committee, it is necessary to review the elements that have been found essential to the successful conduct of the committee's task. These may be summarized under two headings, planning and performance.

First, effective preliminary planning is indispensable. Four component parts must be kept in view. The committee's function must be carefully defined and its terms of reference announced in unmistakable language. All other aspects of the committee's work should then be planned with its task in mind. The appointment of members should be thoughtfully considered. Cabinet officials, and heads of executive agencies in general, should not be appointed unless the problem is so definitely political that the department head must be consulted. Wherever possible, the officials directly concerned with the particular operating problems should be the voting members of the group. In any case, such officials should be given a voice in the committee's deliberations, either as alternates to the political official or in a separate technical board.

The role of the committee staff should be planned in advance of its formal creation. When political officials are appointed to the central committee, the permanent administrator will necessarily play an important role in the executive secretariat. It may be that each committee member will be able to have a great deal of preliminary work done inside his own agency, so that he can come to committee meetings fully equipped with data. In such instances there will be little need for the committee itself to build up a staff. Where the interdepartmental problem is a continuing one, it will not be possible to rely exclusively on individual members' preparation for meetings. Staff members may then be contributed by the constituent departments, or appointments may be specially made to build up the new secretariat. An executive secretary is always needed. By designating one of the department head's staff aides as executive secretary for all committees responsible to the department head, and similarly designating an official from the President's secretariat for all other committees, responsibility of the committee to the central authority could easily be made effective. Finally, the chairman of the committee should be chosen with a view to obtaining an individual who will command respect within the group, partly through the prestige of his office but even more on account of his personal characteristics.

Second, experience has shown that certain aspects of procedure are important to the success of the interdepartmental committee. The members themselves, through their discussions, have one sort of contribution to make. It is elementary to urge that the spirit of departmentalism be suppressed in favor of a cooperative, even conciliatory, attitude. It is also fundamental that discussion be held to the point. A department's position should be stated at the outset by its representative, so that the issues will be clear. From then on, the effort should be made to narrow the issue by means of discussion; in a problem of jurisdiction, to find the specific points of conflict. On the other hand, committee meetings should also be used to discuss larger issues of policy, combining the knowledge gained from departmental operations with viewpoints embracing the whole range of the administration. These two desiderata are all that should be expected from discussion meetings.

The rest of the work must be done by the secretariat. It has a dual role. A large amount of fact-gathering will be essential; in addition, a good deal of creative effort will be necessary if there is to be genuine coordination. Often the factual data may be compiled within the constituent departments. This is the general rule with interdepartmental committees in Great Britain.[9] Whether this method is followed, or whether the fact-gathering is done by a staff specially attached to the com-

9 See W. Ivor Jennings, *Cabinet Government* (The Macmillan Company, New York City, 1937), Chap. VI.

mittee, it will be the task of the executive secretary to assemble the facts in memorandum form for the committee members. Meanwhile, the executive secretary must himself have digested this data so thoroughly that he will recognize all the issues before the committee and be aware of all the implications and overtones of the particular interdepartmental problem. If in addition he has a keen sense of the personal relationships involved, he will be able to contribute in still greater measure to the coordinating process. Once he has reached this point, the executive secretary will have several alternative modes of action. He may confer individually with the committe members, gradually reconciling their viewpoints. He may, with the chairman, divide the group into subcommittees in such a way that the problem will be resolved segment by segment. Finally, he may draw up such interdepartmental agreements as will cover the committee's problems, and by introducing these in a tactful manner indicate to the group the possible lines of agreement. Naturally, the secretary's tactics will vary with the particular task assigned to the interdepartmental committee. The points outlined are, however, the fundamentals of creative staff work.

It has been impossible to do more than describe a selected few of the interdepartmental committees which have been used between 1932 and 1936. If all the committees were minutely examined, practically every important problem confronting the administration during this period would be involved. For the committees which have been listed in this chapter, there are written records of the original authorization, the task assigned, the membership, and in a very few cases minutes and reports. All this, however, does not tell whether coordination was really accomplished, nor describe the methods used. To understand the problems involved it would be necessary to trace the committees back behind the point of origin to the underlying differences they were expected to adjust. To get a clear picture of the issues, to understand the implications of the decisions taken, and to trace the effects of decisions, one would have to sit at the elbow of each administrator in turn for a long period of time. Moreover, the picture is constantly changing. A specific situation may have altered completely by the time the description is put on paper. Finally, no useful purpose would be served by chronicling the activities of all interdepartmental committees. The operations of those which have been listed but not described may be assumed to differ in no significant way from the operations of those committees which have been described in detail in this study.

Among the more general problems of coordination, two are especially relevant to a study of interdepartmental committees. First, what would be the effect on the coordinating process if the civil service were put on a career basis? It seems clear that the establishment of a career service would make the coordinating process far more smooth and even automatic. This conclusion is reinforced by a glance at those interdepartmental committees in our own national administration in which we have something like a career bureaucracy—the army and navy coordinating committees. The Joint Board and Joint Planning Committee, which are the chief organs for planning defense strategy, are headed by the top-ranking officers of the Army General Staff and the Navy Office of Naval Operations. A number of subsidiary technical committees are used for the actual framing of joint plans. It is considered a great advantage by the defense departments that the officers who serve on the Joint Board and its auxiliary planning committees have worked together for a long time. Those officers who are approximately the same age and rank have been detailed at approximately the same time to the Army and Navy war colleges. The traditions of those institutions embody viewpoints common to both services, and such viewpoints become part of the officer's unconscious habits of mind. Working up through the General Staff and the Office of Naval Operations together, their mental set has been reinforced by application of the traditional viewpoint to specific problems of tactics and strategy. As a consequence of long-continued personal association, officers in both services have similar ideas. They have scarcely any difficulty in framing joint plans.

On the other hand, the most frequent criticism of the system is that it tends to perpetuate the traditions of military strategy established by American participation in wars outside United States territory. Recognition in the General Staff is said to come chiefly or solely to those officers whose ideas follow the traditional pattern. Thus the Joint Board continues to draw its plans largely on an expeditionary basis, and ideas for a defense strategy confined to the American continent are not seriously considered. A second important line of criticism is that there can be no effective civilian control of defense policy with this closely-knit type of military bureaucracy. Despite these objections, the mechanism affords an obvious analogy for horizontal integration in the civil departments. If we had a career civil service, the process of coordination would undoubtedly be much simplified. Would the free development of ideas and intelligence in general be impeded? And would there be less control by political officials over the formation of policy? The present study suggests that questions such as these are not the most serious problems confronting our administrative system.

Our experience with interdepartmental committees reveals a graver danger—the inability of our present administrative organization to survey the national economy as a whole and to achieve unified action in dealing with national problems. Consequently, the need for a career civil service cannot be too strongly emphasized. Unfortunately, the prospect of achieving this in the United States is remote. The anxiety of democratic leaders to reassure their constitutents of the vitality of a free government makes them lean over backwards to avoid the appearance of strongly centralized executive power. Progress in administrative efficiency is attacked as undue aggrandizement. Officials anxious to keep their own status in government bureaus, and vocational interests fearful of their ability to gain their ends under a strong government, are quick to pick up the argument and turn it into political propaganda. Nevertheless, it is a major conclusion of this study that coordination can never be really effective without fundamental improvements in our civil service.

The question then arises, to what extent is consistency in administration possible or desirable, and what contribution in general can be expected from the interdepartmental committee? The need for a fluent sort of consistency emerges ever more urgently as one of the greatest problems confronting the modern state. A realistic approach to the problem of coordination will accept the premise that it is necessary to recognize limits to the consistency of governmental action under modern economic conditions. So long as we continue to believe that conflicting occupational interests should be placated rather than coerced, government will have to steer its course on a rather pragmatic basis. Complete reconciliation of all interests will be impossible; agreements can only be temporary and imperfect. Moreover, as government moves through different phases of a program, a later decision may cancel out an earlier. Contingency must be counted as an important factor in both legislative and administrative planning.

The lack of consistency may simply result from a failure to survey the situation and plan a course of action to fit the facts as nearly as is practicable. The legislation may not have been thought out at some one point. This may be remedied by improving the machinery for organizing intelligence. Here, an interdepartmental committee may be very useful. But governmental policy may be inconsistent because of broadly political or social reasons. Possibly we cannot afford the luxury of consonance. The President, for example, is not only obliged to unify his legislative proposals; as leader of a political party, he must also hold together what in essence is rarely more than a coalition. Thus it is necessary for him to satisfy conflicting vocational interests. He cannot be rigorously consistent; he is constrained to compromise. The most we should expect is that the Administration, looking at its political situation and watching the indirect effects of all its measures, will at least be conscious of its compromises. In doing this, cross-sectional consultative machinery will be important, even essential, but its use will not be a guarantee of consistency.

In brief, where discrepancies exist but have not been recognized, an interdepartmental committee may bring them out and may offer a method of resolving the administrative dissonance. It would be fatuous to look for complete accord from an interdepartmental committee, but this should be the general ideal and specific objective of every such group. Thus, the interdepartmental committee may mitigate the effects of inconsistency in administration, though it cannot remove the cause.

BIBLIOGRAPHY

I. Theory and Practice of Administrative Management

Alford, L. P., *Management's Handbook* (The Ronald Press, New York, 1924).

Beckerath, Herbert von, *Modern Industrial Organization* (trans. by R. Newcomb and F. Krebs, McGraw-Hill Book Co., New York, 1933).

Brady, Robert A., *The Rationalization Movement in German Industry* (University of California Press, Berkeley, 1933).

Burrows, Harry R., *The Problems and Practice of Economic Planning* (P. S. King and Sons, London, 1937).

Creedy, Frederick, *Human Nature in Business* (E. Benn, Ltd., London, 1927).

Dimock, Marshall E., *Modern Politics and Administration; A Study of the Creative State* (American Book Co., New York, 1937).

Fayol, Henri, *Industrial and General Administration* (trans. by J. A. Coubrough, International Management Association, Geneva, 1936).

Florence, Philip Sargent, *The Logic of Industrial Organization* (K. Paul, Trench, Trubner and Co., Ltd., London, 1933).

Follett, M. P., *Creative Experience* (Longmans, Green and Co., New York, 1924).

Gaus, J. M., White, L. D., and Dimock, M. E., *The Frontiers of Public Administration* (University of Chicago Press, Chicago, 1936).

Gulick, L., and Urwick, L. (eds.), *Papers on the Science of Administration* (Institute of Public Administration, New York, 1937).

Herring, E. Pendleton, *Public Administration and the Public Interest* (McGraw-Hill Book Co., New York, 1936).

Lansburgh, B. H., *Industrial Management* (J. Wiley and Sons, New York, 1928).

Meriam, Lewis, *Public Service and Special Training* (University of Chicago Press, 1936).

Ministry of Reconstruction, Great Britain, *Report of the Machinery of Government Committee* (H. M. Stationery Office, London, 1918).

Mooney, James D., and Reiley, Alan C., *Onward, Industry!* (Harper and Bros., New York, 1931).

Mosher, W. E., and Kingsley, J. Donald, *Public Personnel Administration* (Harper and Bros., New York, 1935).

Person, H. (ed.), *Scientific Management in American Industry* (Taylor Society, New York, 1929).

Rogers, Lindsay, *Social Science and National Planning* (mimeographed, Social Science Research Council, Washington, D. C., 1934).

Schell, Erwin, *The Technique of Executive Control* (McGraw-Hill Book Co., New York, 1935).

Sheldon, O., *The Philosophy of Management* (I. Pitman and Sons, London, 1923).

Taylor, F. W., *Principles of Scientific Management* (Harper and Bros., New York, 1923).

Tead, Ordway, *Human Nature and Management* (McGraw-Hill Book Co., New York, 1929).

——, *The Art of Leadership* (Whittlesey House, McGraw-Hill Book Co., New York, 1935).

——, and Metcalf, Henry C., *Personnel Administration* (3rd ed., McGraw-Hill Book Co., New York, 1933).

Urwick, Lyndall, *Committees in Organization* (Terminal House, London, 1938).

——, *Management of Tomorrow* (Nisbet and Co., London, 1923).

——, *Organization as a Technical Problem* (International Management Institute, Geneva, 1933).

——, *The Meaning of Rationalisation* (Nisbet and Co., London, 1929).

Various Authors, *Critical Essays on Scientific Management* (Taylor Society, New York, 1925).

Wallas, Graham, *The Great Society* (Macmillan Co., New York, 1919).

White, Leonard D., *Government Career Service* (University of Chicago Press, Chicago, 1935).

White, Leonard D., Bland, C. H., Sharp, W. R., and Marx, F. M., *Civil Service Abroad* (Commission of Inquiry on Public Service Personnel, McGraw-Hill Book Co., New York, 1935).

Chamberlain, J. P., "Democratic Control of Administration," *American Bar Association Journal*, Vol. 3 (1927), pp. 186-188.

Clark, Sir Geoffrey, "Business Management of the Public Service," *Public Administration*, Vol. VIII, No. 1 (January, 1930).

Clark, Wallace, "A Control Chart for the Chief Executive," *The Iron Age*,

——, "American Management in Europe," *Mechanical Engineering*, Vol. 52, No. 12 (December, 1930).

——, "How a Planning Department was Organized," *Business*, November, 1932.

——, "The Outside Management Consultant," *Industry Illustrated.*

Craven, T. T., "Coordination in Public Administration," *Taylor Society Bulletin*, Vol. 27 (April, 1932), pp. 71-86.

Dimock, Marshall E., "Executive Responsibilities," *Journal of the Society for the Advancement of Management*, Vol. III, No. 1 (January, 1938).

Feldman, Herman, "A Personnel Program for the Federal Civil Service," House Doc. 773, 71st Congress, 3rd Session (1931).

Ferguson, Homer, "A Plea for Inefficiency in Government," *Nation's Business*, November, 1928, p. 20.

Finer, Herman, "Better Government Personnel; America's Next Frontier," *Political Science Quarterly*, Vol. 51 (December, 1936), pp. 569-599.

Follett, M. P., "The Illusion of Final Authority," *Taylor Society Bulletin*, Vol. 11 (December, 1936), pp. 243-256.

Macmahon, Arthur W., "Boards, Advisory," *Encyclopedia of the Social Sciences*, Vol. 2, pp. 609-611.

Parker, Graham W., "Training Men for Management," *Industry Illustrated.*

Turner, Jennie M., "Democracy in Administration," *American Political Science Review*, Vol. XVII (May, 1923), pp. 216-230.

Urwick, Lyndall, "Executive Decentralization with Functional Coordination," *Management Review*, December, 1935, pp. 355 ff.

Various Authors, "Efficiency as an Alternative to Control," *Public Administration*, Vol. VI, No. 2 (April, 1928).

White, Leonard D., "Can We Improve the Public Service?" *Yale Review*, Vol. 25 (December, 1935), pp. 277-290.

II. Executive Control in the National Government

Commission of Inquiry on Public Service Personnel, *Report and Minutes of Evidence* (McGraw-Hill Book Co., New York, 1935).

Elliott, William Yandell, *The Need for Constitutional Reform* (Whittlesey House, McGraw-Hill Book Co., New York, 1935), Part I.

Friedrich, Carl Joachim, *Constitutional Government and Politics* (Harper and Bros., New York, 1937), Chaps. XIV, XX.

——, *et al.*, *Problems of the American Public Service* (Commission of Inquiry on Public Service Personnel, McGraw-Hill Book Co., New York, 1935).

Greer, Sarah, *A Bibliography of Civil Service and Personnel Administration* (McGraw-Hill Book Co., New York, 1935).

Hart, James, *The President and Federal Administration*, in *Essays on the Law and Practice of Governmental Administration* (Dimock, M. E., and Haines, C. G., eds., Johns Hopkins Press, Baltimore, 1935).

Macmahon, Arthur W., and Millett, J. D., *Federal Administrators* (Columbia University Press, New York, 1939).

President's Committee on Administrative Management, *Report and Special Studies* (U. S. Government Printing Office, Washington, D. C., 1937).

Schmeckebier, L. F., *New Federal Organizations; An Outline of their Structure and Functions* (Brookings Institution, Washington, D. C., 1934).

Spicer, George W., *From Political Chief to Administrative Chief*, in *Essays on the Law and Practice of Governmental Administration* (Dimock, M. E., and Haines, C. G., eds., Johns Hopkins Press, Baltimore, 1935).

Thomas, Norman, and Sargent, Noel, *Must We Reorganize for Recovery?* (American Book Co., New York, 1935).

Weber, Gustavus A., *Organized Efforts for the Improvement of Methods of Administration in the United States* (1919).

Woody, Carroll H., *The Growth of the Federal Government, 1915-1932* (McGraw-Hill Book Co., New York, 1934).

Culp, M. S., "Executive Power in Emergencies," *Michigan Law Review*, Vol. 31 (June, 1933), pp. 1066-1096.

Herring, E. Pendleton, "Social Forces and the Reorganization of the Federal Bureaucracy," *Southwestern Social Science Quarterly*, Vol. 15 (December, 1934), pp. 185-200.

Hurt, Peyton, "Who Should Reorganize the National Administration?" *American Political Science Review*, Vol. 26 (December, 1932), pp. 1082-1098.

Kendall, H. P., "The Problem of the Chief Executive," *Bulletin of the Taylor Society*, Vol. 7, No. 2 (April, 1922).

Rogers, Lindsay, "Cabinet," *Encyclopedia of the Social Sciences*, Vol. 3, pp. 1932-1934.

Shumate, Roger V., "Development of National Administration in the United States, 1932-1935," *American Political Science Review*, Vol. 29 (October, 1935), pp. 853-856.

Various Authors, "Proposal for a Service of General Administration in the Government of the United States," *Public Personnel Studies*, Vol. 7 December, 1929), pp. 166-179.

III. Administrative Coordination in the New Deal

Brown, Douglass V., *et al.*, *The Economics of the Recovery Program* (McGraw-Hill Book Co., New York, 1934).

Burns, Eveline M., *Toward Social Security* (McGraw-Hill Book Co., New York, 1936).

Central Statistical Board, *Annual Reports* (Washington, D. C., 1934 to 1939).

Committee on Economic Security, *Social Security in America* (Social Security Board, Washington, D. C., 1937).

Dickinson, John, *et al.*, *America's Recovery Program* (Oxford University Press, New York, 1934).

Douglas, Paul H., *Social Security in the United States* (McGraw-Hill Book Co., New York, 1936).

Johnson, Hugh, S., *The Blue Eagle from Egg to Earth* (Doubleday, Doran and Co., Garden City, New York, 1935).

Kent, Frank R., *Without Gloves* (William Morrow Co., New York, 1934).

Landis, Benson Y., *Must the Nation Plan?* (Association Press, New York, 1934).

Lyon, Leverett S., *et al.*, *The National Recovery Administration* (Brookings Institution, Washington, D. C., 1935).

National Organization for Public Health Nursing, *Survey of Public Health Nursing* (Commonwealth Fund, New York, 1934).

National Advisory Committee on Aeronautics, *Annual Reports* (Washington, D. C., 1921 to 1939).

Nourse, E. G., Davis, J. S., and Black, J. D., *Three Years of the AAA* (Brookings Institution, Washington, D. C., 1936).

Sayre, Francis B., *America Must Act* (World Peace Foundation, Boston, 1936).

Schumpeter, J. A., *et al.*, *The Economics of the Recovery Program* (McGraw-Hill Book Co., New York, 1934).

Stolberg, Benjamin, and Vinton, Warren Jay, *The Economic Consequences of the New Deal* (Harcourt, Brace and Co., New York, 1935).

Stone, W. T., *The Administration of the Department of State* (Foreign Policy Association Information Service, Supplement No. 9, February, 1929).

Stowell, Ellery C., *The Economic Adviser of the Department of State* (Digest Press, Washington, D. C., 1935).

Wallace, Schuyler C., *The New Deal in Action* (Harper and Bros., New York, 1934).

Williamson, Rene deV., *The Politics of Planning in the Oil Industry under the Codes* (Harper and Bros., New York, 1936).

Elliott, William Y., "The Economics of the Recovery Program," *American Political Science Review*, Vol. XXVIII, No. 3 (June, 1934), pp. 410-423.

Lorwin, Lewis L., "Social Aspects of the Planning State," *American Political Science Review*, Vol. 29 (February, 1934), pp. 16-22.

Merriam, Charles E., "A Closer View of the Machinery of Control," *Plan Age*, January, 1936, pp. 9-16.

Post, S. Lyle, "Coordination of National Administration," *American Political Science Review*, Vol. 29 (April, 1935), pp. 269-274.

Rankin, R. S., "The Presidency under the New Deal," *South Atlantic Quarterly*, Vol. 33 (April, 1934), pp. 152-164.

Smith, John W. B., "The Government's Housing Program to Date," *American Bar Association Journal*, September, 1936.

INDEX